The Mimbres
People

NEW ASPECTS OF ANTIQUITY

General Editor: COLIN RENFREW

Consulting Editor for the Americas: JEREMY A. SABLOFF

STEVEN A. LEBLANC

The Mimbres People

Ancient Pueblo Painters of the American Southwest

with 129 illustrations, 15 in colour

THAMES AND HUDSON

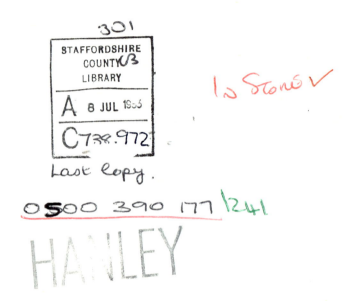
Printed and bound in the German Democratic Republic
by Interdruck, Leipzig

Contents

General Editor's foreword

There are in the world only a few art styles which possess the ability to seize our attention by the sheer force of the visual impact of their products, and then to hold it while successive subtleties of the work reveal themselves to us. The painted pottery known to us today by the name 'Mimbres' is one of these: it cries out across the centuries, from museum showcase or art collection, with its own peculiar clarity and coherence.

When I first saw examples of Mimbres Ware some fifteen years ago, I was forcibly struck by the qualities of zest and vitality and above all simplicity which for me set it apart from many of the more elaborate, perhaps more sophisticated works of art of Mesoamerica. And I was curious to know what special conjunction of circumstances had come together to produce, in one rather restricted area of the North American Southwest, an art style so distinctive and so immediately appealing.

At that time there was no clear answer to such a question – most of the pots in private collections and museum reserves were from private, amateur digging operations with no adequate record of their context. There was an enigma here – and one stemming largely from what is now regarded as the haphazard and irresponsible looting of the American archaeological heritage, even if forty years ago it may have seemed relatively harmless 'pothunting'.

This question, and the underlying issue of archaeological responsibility also troubles Steven LeBlanc, who acted energetically to do something effective about *both*. He was able to rescue and re-interpret such records as remained of early excavations, for instance at the Galaz site, and by re-excavating there, and undertaking an energetic campaign at a number of other sites, to establish a coherent time-scale for Mimbres archaeology.

In doing so he has been able to rescue much of the human context in which these pots were made, so that 'Mimbres' means not only a pottery style, but a whole complex of finds, both architecture and artifacts – a whole 'Culture', if one likes to use that archaeological jargon term. Unfortunately the difficult conditions of work, in the wake of so much looting and destruction, make the social structure more difficult to recover. Much has been irretrievably lost. Yet we can now begin to glimpse a society that was not centrally organized to any marked extent. Nor was widespread craft specialization an important feature of the economic structure. At first sight this seems to the modern eye rather surprising, in view of the great mastery shown in the shaping and especially the painting of the pots. LeBlanc has also begun the difficult task of defining the main elements of the visual 'language' of the painted decoration, and of investigating the artistic conventions which no doubt underlie the impression of great coherence which it gives.

Steven LeBlanc has tackled the problem of pothunting in a practical way by setting up a trust, the Mimbres Foundation, to take into ownership and hence protection as many sites as possible of those that remain. For it is a sad deficiency of United States law that virtually no protection is offered to archaeological sites, however important, unless they are on public land. The owner of an important site is free to destroy it if he wishes, whether to obtain any pots and other objects which it may contain, or for any other reason. The lead in this matter taken by the Mimbres Foundation has now been followed by a comparable organization, but one of wider scope: the Archaeological Conservancy. Its objective is to acquire and preserve the most significant sites in the United States. The author is a member of its board of directors.

This is an important book. It reports the rescue from destruction and oblivion of materials crucial to our understanding of one of the major art styles of the non-urban world: certainly of one of the great artistic achievements of the Americas. And it highlights both the recent sad neglect of a rich national heritage and the success which a determined group of people can have through their concerted work to counter that neglect.

Colin Renfrew

Consulting Editor's foreword

Tourists who visit the North American Southwest today are inevitably impressed by the large Pueblo ruins at Chaco Canyon or Mesa Verde. The ancestors of the modern Pueblo peoples who built these sites have been named Anasazi by archaeologists who have undertaken considerable research at Anasazi sites. However, much less attention has been paid to the ancient peoples who lived to the south of the Anasazi and inhabited the southwest portion of modern-day New Mexico and the southeastern part of modern-day Arizona. These latter peoples, who lived in this region from just before the time of Christ, have been labelled Mogollon (pronounced 'muggy-own') by archaeologists. While their architectural remains are not nearly as spectacular as those of their Anasazi neighbors to the north, at least one Mogollon group, known as the Mimbres culture to archaeologists, produced a fascinating painted pottery which has great appeal to modern aesthetic senses.

The recent research of Steven LeBlanc and his colleagues has given us a clearer picture of Mimbres culture than has heretofore been available. In this book, Dr LeBlanc offers professionals, students, and lay readers alike a new glimpse into the nature of ancient Mimbres culture, its development through time, and its changing adaptations to the relatively arid uplands of New Mexico and Arizona. In outlining the different aspects of Mimbres culture which his archaeological research has revealed, Dr LeBlanc also helps to dispel a persistent impression of pre-industrial societies which used to have significant strength among professional archaeologists and still remains a part of popular views. In its simplest form, this view of ancient groups sees a number of cultural traits as being inextricably linked through time. For example, it used to be thought that there was a whole constellation of cultural traits which characterized urban civilizations of the past. In fact, lists of traits were formulated and were used to define such cultural developments. But as archaeological research expanded globally in the mid-twentieth century, it soon became clear that there was no hard and fast list which could definitively characterize urban civilizations, or other cultural developments for that matter. Writing, for instance, which was once thought of as the *sine qua non* of ancient civilizations was shown to be absent in certain cases, such as the Inca of South America, which in most other respects looked like and functioned as complex civilizations. Other research has shown that large numbers of people and complex bureaucratic organizations are not needed to build huge structures or monuments. Dr LeBlanc's studies, which he reports on here in this work, make a similar point by showing how Mimbres people with a non-complex culture (no class system, bureaucracies, standing armies, writing, or the like) were able to invent a sophisticated art style while attempting to make the most of a relatively difficult environment. Dr LeBlanc's clear, jargon-free description of various aspects of Mimbres culture allows readers to appreciate its major achievement in pottery production while at the same time placing this achievement in the context of the total cultural system of the Mimbres people. The picture of the growth of Mimbres culture in its overall environment painted by Steven LeBlanc should help bring this oft-neglected group to public attention and permit readers to see Mimbres pottery not just as isolated pieces of art but as part of a functioning and developing ancient culture.

Jeremy A. Sabloff

1 A new approach to a difficult problem

The Mimbres culture of southwestern New Mexico has long been considered   *fig. 1*
unique among prehistoric North American cultures because of its lively,
figurative art. These paintings, done on the inside of hemispherical bowls, are
in both geometric and representational styles, but it is the naturalistic figures
which so capture us today. Mimbres bowls have held a fascination for
archaeologists and art lovers alike, but as a result they have led to the looting
of Mimbres settlement sites on a scale unequalled in the United States. The
bowls are found within the domestic structures themselves, so digging for
them destroys the very heart of the remains of the villages of their makers.

The Mimbres people lived in an area of some 13,000 sq miles in New Mexico   *fig. 2*
and seem to have been most concentrated along a small river – in other less
arid regions it would be called a stream – the Rio Mimbres. This river, only 3 m
wide and 1 m deep, and the valley of the same name through which it flows,
have given their name to this prehistoric people. The Mimbres River was so
called by the early Spanish settlers because of the small willows or *mimbres*
which are found along its banks. The same name was applied at the turn of the
century to the culture of the people who lived along the river and produced the
famous bowls.

The first significant archaeological research began in the 1920s, producing
numerous examples of the characteristic pottery, as well as house foundations
and other material objects. Until recently, surprisingly little else was known
about the Mimbres. Several important unanswered questions remained. What
were the origins of the distinctive pottery? Why did it abruptly disappear from
the archaeological record? Did the Mimbres people die out or did they become
assimilated into other cultural groups? Equally important was the timing of
these events. When did the Mimbres and their pottery disappear? Was it
during the great drought of the late 1200s when so many other groups
vanished from the archaeological record in the Southwest? Or was it earlier
and due to different causes? These and other questions have long made the
Mimbres area an important one for archaeology.

As interesting as these questions were and as exciting as we hoped the
answers to be, the Mimbres Foundation, the work of which is the focus of this
book, did not begin a research program solely because of these interests. As a
result of their high value in today's primitive-art market, Mimbres village sites   plate 8
have been massively looted. At the turn of the century pick and shovel only

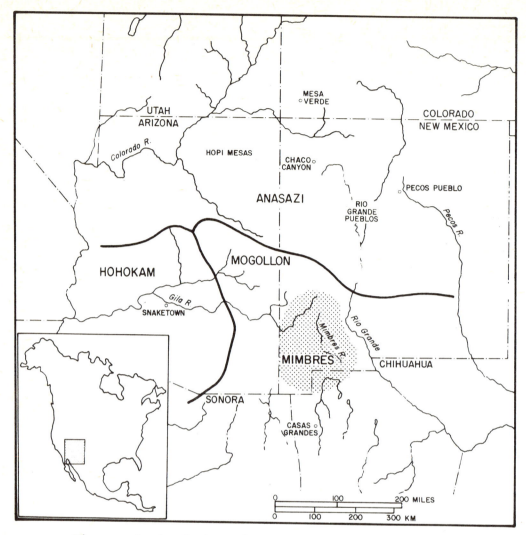

1 The greater American Southwest, showing the three major cultural subdivisions and the location of the Mimbres area.

plate 7   were used, but in the early 1960s a method of bulldozing the sites was developed which did not destroy all the pottery. This technological 'advance' led to a much more rapid and complete devastation of village sites. It was quite obvious that, if something was not done soon, all the Mimbres sites would be obliterated and nothing further could be learned about these people.

    Unlike most archaeology in the United States, the Mimbres project was not the result of a University or other public organization using federal funds to undertake field research. Instead the impetus came from the art community. Most serious collectors of Mimbres pottery had little knowledge of Mimbres archaeology and even less of the level of site destruction. But, when made

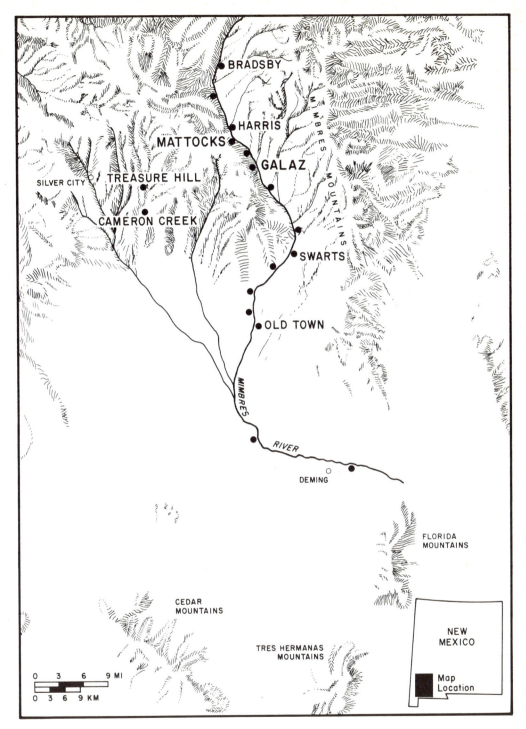

2 *The Mimbres Valley area. The major Mimbres villages are shown as black dots, with those mentioned in the text labeled. Modern towns are shown as open circles.*

aware of the seriousness of the situation, the vast majority were only too willing to help. Thus the initial work was financed entirely by private donations from people connected with the arts, and most of our remaining work was also supported in this manner, although supplementary grants were made available by the government. In fact it was the vision of one man, Tony Berlant that really made all the rest possible. An artist in his own right, Tony Berlant is also well known as a leading expert on Navajo blankets. He recognized the artistic worth of Mimbres pottery and began collecting pieces. When I subsequently explained to him the terrifying level of destruction, he took it upon himself to persuade others in the art community that something needed to be done to try and learn something about the Mimbres people before all the village sites disappeared. Fortunately, he convinced Edwin Janss of this need, and an initial grant from the Janss Foundation enabled us to begin work in the Mimbres Valley.

Our initial reconnaissance of the area in 1973 was very discouraging. Most of the sites we visited seemed hopelessly disturbed. Although we later learned that such remains could yield great quantities of information, we were very pessimistic at first. This was intensified by the reactions of other archaeologists. Many felt the situation was almost hopeless and that the sites in the Mimbres Valley proper were essentially gone.

Fortunately, the belief held by most archaeologists that damaged sites are of little use is based on the concept of archaeological context. That is, artifacts have only limited information themselves, and it is the context of their discovery which is most enlightening. If a site has been severely interfered with, much of the contextual information is invariably lost. As archaeology is an expensive and time-consuming activity, working where deposits are likely to have been disturbed is correctly seen as inefficient and wasteful. If, however, one is confronted with a culture which is primarily represented by such remains, one has no choice; we had to find a way to surmount the problem.

At this point we met up with Robert McAnally, who owned three major sites in the Mimbres Valley. He had not been aware of their scientific importance and in fact had recently permitted looting to go on. He quickly accepted our arguments, however, and made the sites available to us, ultimately, as we shall see, making it possible for us to protect the ruins permanently

Our initial goal was to discover how much information could still be gained from sites that had been dug by pothunters. Unfortunately, archaeologists in the United States and elsewhere have generally avoided sites that have been severely looted and we had almost no experience to guide us. Thus our first field season was one of both frustration and important learning.

The looting of major sites such as the Mattocks ruin had taken place over a long period of time. Holes had been refilled and compacted, so that it was in many cases not possible to determine where previous digging had taken place. We began working in the traditional manner. We would lay out an excavation

unit and excavate in fine levels, screening all material as we went. We recovered quantities of prehistoric materials from soil that appeared stratified. After carrying on like this for a couple of days we would reach a depth where we should have encountered the floor of a prehistoric room, but instead of retrieving Mimbres artifacts we would find horseshoes, tin cans, and other historic material. We would then realize the room had been dug into fifty or seventy years earlier. Some historic material had been left behind by the diggers, while the earth that they had removed, still containing artifacts, would slowly fall back into the hole. After the earth had once again been compacted it was almost impossible to determine that the deposits had previously been disturbed.

This came as a shock. We fully expected to find such pillaged rooms, but we assumed we would easily be able to recognize them when digging began. We tried every kind of technique. In one case, we deliberately excavated an area we knew to be disturbed – we had a photograph taken by the people who dug the hole showing exactly where they had worked. The soil appeared to be as clearly stratified and compact as we had ever encountered in undisturbed sites. This realization left us depressed, and for a while we were uncertain how to proceed. Fortunately we discovered an important behavior pattern of the looters. They always dug up the floor of rooms in their search for bowls. Thus we determined that a small test pit could quickly tell us if the floor of a room was intact. Only if we found such a floor could we be sure the room warranted excavation in its entirety.

At the end of the first two months in 1974 we had excavated a large number of previously dug areas, but had also discovered how to locate undisturbed zones and had found some important deposits. Moreover, we had learned how to recover important information even from the plundered areas, so that no matter what kind of chaos we encountered, we could learn something. In particular, we discovered that charcoal specimens were not removed by looters, and, although they were no longer in situ, were apparently not far from their original location. These botanical remains proved invaluable because many could be dated by the tree-ring method (which will be discussed below). Surprisingly, we could now accurately date rooms that had been totally looted. Another important aspect of our early research was the identification of other prehistoric cultures in the valley. These had gone unrecognized by previous archaeologists and would be helpful in understanding the origins and demise of the Mimbres people. Thus the stage was set for four additional years of field work – between 1975 and 1978 – which have led to a better understanding of Mimbres culture and of those which preceded and followed it.

During these five field seasons we conducted excavations on twenty-seven sites. This is not a typical archaeological strategy, where work is usually concentrated on one or at most a few sites. Our decision to work on a broad spectrum was based on several factors. Of major importance was the knowledge that although archaeologists had worked in the area before (and the Southwest of the US possesses without a doubt the best-dated prehistoric sequence in the world), we knew surprisingly little about the sequence of events in the valley. In order to develop a good chronology it was important to excavate on a number of sites from various periods.

As a case in point, we would be certain of the end date of the Mimbres people only by finding, excavating, and dating sites of the people that followed them. Similar excavations on earlier sites helped establish the origins and development of the Classic Mimbres culture.

A practical consideration was also at work. Because the Mimbres sites were so badly looted, it was difficult to find large, contiguous, undisturbed areas. These are necessary if archaeologists are to work out the social dynamics of groups within the communities, to understand the use of space in these sites, and how they grew and declined as communities. Such deposits were very difficult to locate and in many cases nonexistent. Consequently we had little hope of succeeding in such an approach. There was little use in working on the internal structure of a single site. Instead, the study of the relationships between sites seemed to be a more fruitful approach. It required the systematic survey of large areas, both to locate sites to excavate and to help understand how they were related to each other.

Fortunately, such an approach allowed us to analyze the settlement patterns of the region and the fluctuations in population over time. The regional perspective also enabled us to examine how Mimbres pottery functioned within the society as a whole, and not just how it was used at a single site. To some extent all archaeology is a compromise. One can never do all one would hope for, even in the best of circumstances. There were approaches we wished we could have taken, but which were impossible given the condition of the sites. However, once we had accepted these facts, there was a surprising amount that could still be learned.

The results of these five seasons of archaeology produced results that far exceeded our initial expectations, primarily in ways we never invisaged when we began. On the archaeological front we produced the first solid chronology for the area. This chronology, as we shall see, was quite unexpected, and it and other work has led to a broad understanding of what happened to the Mimbres people – a previously totally baffling problem. We also discovered that the Mimbres had a rich and important ceremonial architectural tradition that had a much longer history and was much more elaborate than had previously been perceived. But beyond these archaeological advances, there were some other consequences that are perhaps even more far-reaching.

Archaeologists are used to working with potsherds, mainly because that is usually what they recover. It is only in a few areas such as the Aegean and coastal Peru that considerable quantities of complete vessels have been recovered. In these regions archaeologists and art historians have made use of the vessels, but they were rarely able to do so in the case of the Mimbres.

Literally thousands of Mimbres bowls had been recovered and were potentially available for study. Although a majority had lost their archaeological context because they had been looted, this still constituted an enormous wealth of information.

We began to photograph all the examples of Mimbres bowls we could find, even though this was not in the tradition of North American archaeology. In fact, more than one archaeologist remarked that what we were doing was not archaeology at all, but art history. To an extent this was true, and in fact it was a grant from the National Endowment of Arts which turned our informal effort into a systematic attempt to photograph all extant Mimbres bowls. This has resulted in the Mimbres Archive housed at the Maxwell Museum of the University of New Mexico. At the present time, over 6500 bowls have been photographed. Most surprising and helpful was the fact that information about where a great number of these bowls came from had been preserved, so that the bowl photos were even more useful than we originally suspected.

Much of what we learned about the Mimbres has, directly or indirectly, been a result of the development of this archive. This should serve as a reminder to all archaeologists that information on the past is available from a wide spectrum of sources; it is up to us to discover these sources and to learn how to use them. To a large degree the Mimbres project was really the implementation of this concept. We had to discover how to excavate sites that most others considered hopelessly destroyed, and we also had to find out how to learn from the results of previous work in the region that was done in ways considerably different from today's archaeology. We also needed to analyze the Mimbres bowls themselves, even though some believed they had become archaeologically useless and simply pieces of art.

Finally, we realized that while excavation of these sites could recover new information today, there was a danger that no sites would remain intact for researchers with new and as yet undiscovered techniques to study. In order to preserve part of the Mimbres culture for perpetuity, the Mimbres Foundation acquired several remaining sites in the valley, an approach rarely taken in the United States by a non-governmental organization.

My goal here is to place the Mimbres culture and its art traditions in the context of the prehistory of the Southwest. Of particular concern is the development of the pottery-painting style and the question of the ultimate demise of the Mimbres people. At the same time I want to show how the Mimbres project proceeded to do research in an area so badly looted that others thought further work useless, and how we came to learn what we did.

2 The prehistoric farming peoples of the Southwest

The Mimbres people were one of many prehistoric groups to inhabit the arid American Southwest. Fortunately for archaeologists, there are today Indian tribes which are direct descendants of the various prehistoric inhabitants. Thus we are able to gain great insight into the nature of the technology, social organization, and the adaptive strategy of the prehistoric people by drawing analogies with the historic inhabitants of the area.[1]

The American Southwest includes the states of New Mexico and Arizona, as well as the southern parts of Colorado and Utah, and also covers the northern parts of the Mexican states of Chihuahua and Sonora. It is for the most part quite elevated, usually exceeding 1375 m, with some mountains of more than 3650 m. Although it is traversed by many rivers such as the Rio Grande and the Colorado the Southwest is quite dry, with typical annual rainfalls of around 40 cm. Permanent water courses are few. While most of the area is not a true desert, vegetation is generally sparse, consisting mainly of shrub-grasslands or pigmy woodlands, where trees are 3–6 m high and widely spread.

When the Spanish explorers first contacted the indigenous peoples of the
plate 1 Southwest, they found groups of horticulturalists some of whom lived in compact village settlements.[2] Villages, or 'pueblos', were built either of adobe (clay walls left to dry in the sun) or rock, and consisted of contiguous rooms which, on occasion, numbered into hundreds. Sometimes all the rooms were incorporated into a single structure, often surrounding an open court or plaza. In other cases there were several separate blocks in a village. Blocks might contain from only a few to hundreds of rooms, and were frequently multi-storied. Suites of between two and five interconnected rooms were owned by individual families. These pueblos are similar in many ways to today's apartment complexes. Ceremonial rooms were sometimes included in the blocks; others were freestanding and located elsewhere. The Pueblos – village-dwelling Indians – call these ceremonial structures *kivas*, and this name has been applied by archaeologists to the prehistoric ceremonial chambers.

Some early Spanish chronicles provide descriptions of these Pueblo towns. Early in 1591 Castano de Sosa visited the pueblo of Pecos and reported: 'The
plates 2, 3 houses in this pueblo are built like military barracks, back to back, with doors opening out all around; and they are four or five stories high. There are no doors opening into the streets on the ground floors; the houses are entered

18

from above by means of portable hand ladders and trap doors. Each floor of every house has three or four rooms, so that each house, as a whole, counting from top to bottom, has fifteen or sixteen rooms, very neat and well whitewashed. Every house is equipped with facilities for grinding corn, including three or four grinding stones mounted in small troughs and provided with pestles; all is whitewashed. . . .'[3]

The large pueblos the Spaniards found in the 1500s we now know were heirs to a long tradition, the first having been built some six or seven centuries earlier. Prior to that, people throughout the Southwest lived in semi-subterranean structures known as pithouses.

The Indians these Spaniards met were primarily dependent on horticulture, based on the plant triad prevalent in Mesoamerica – maize, beans, and squash. Apparently these crops were never the sole diet either historically or prehistorically. Ethnographic studies in the Southwest have shown that only about 50 per cent of calories actually came from domesticated foods, and wild plants and animals were very important.[4] Deer and rabbits were the animals most often hunted and this was particularly true prehistorically in the Mimbres area. Other animals, including elk, big-horn sheep, antelope, bear, turkey, and waterfowl were also hunted, but these were much less common and at least some were probably processed as much for hides or feathers as for meat.

Wild plants were important food sources, in particular piñon nuts, wild sunflower, and seeds and leaves of amaranthus and chenopodium plants. The stalks and leaves of the yucca and agave were also collected and roasted as were prickly-pear buds. Of course, plants were also used for such things as basketry and soap, while cotton was grown for cloth.

We feel quite secure in using our close ethnographic analogies to interpret the plants, food-procurement and food-processing remains we find in prehistoric sites in the Southwest. However, we cannot be so certain in using extant groups as models for the prehistoric social organization, mainly because we believe that some forms of structure existed then that have not survived. The Puebloan groups encountered by the conquistadores were organizationally more simple than the Aztecs or the peoples in Central Mexico. The fundamental social units were based on kinship. The lineage comprised several generations of direct female descent, while the clan consisted of several lineages, at least fictively all descended from a common ancestor. Although the Spanish, and others that followed, referred to certain individuals as chiefs, such positions were purely temporary, since leadership was not hereditary but earned. Moreover, there was little social or task differentiation in these societies. Indeed, there do not appear to have been any full-time craft specialists. We have identified some apparently sexual division of labor; women certainly were potters and men were weavers. And besides the exchange of goods and foodstuffs, often occurring at ceremonial activities, every household farmed and produced its own basic domestic goods.

plates 4, 5

As in most tribal societies, religion was a major component of life. The leaders were also religious officials, and ceremonial activities regulated the annual cycle. The Puebloan religion was highly concerned with rain, a critical factor in this semi-arid region, as we shall see. It was also a strongly participatory cult with nearly all adult males belonging to religious fraternities obliged to perform both private and public ceremonies for the good of the plate 6   entire group. The ceremonial structures, or kivas, were built to house these fraternities during retreats and certain rituals. Other ceremonies, in particular large Kachina (masked-figure) dances, were held in the open plazas.

It is clear that much of this historically documented social organization had strong parallels in the prehistoric sequence. There is every reason to believe that most of the prehistoric farming groups in the Southwest were similarly structured, and it is clear that religion involving kivas was also involved. In the Mimbres area we find both small buildings which could have held between ten and twenty people and extremely large ones which could have housed up to 200 people. The earliest of them appeared soon after the beginning of the Christian era.

It is dangerous, however, to assume that all societies in the Southwest were similarly organized. Some groups, including the ones that may have eclipsed the Mimbres people, were probably more complex than any encountered by the Spanish. In these cases it is likely that we had true chiefs, who were hereditary, and that full-time craft specialists existed. One of our goals in studying the Mimbres was to determine whether they had social organizations characteristic of modern Puebloan groups in the Southwest, or whether they were somewhat more elaborate.

Chronology

We now know that the American Southwest was occupied for 10,000 years or more. However, almost until the beginning of the Christian era these inhabitants were nomadic hunters and gatherers. Prior to 6000 or 8000 BC they made use of Pleistocene fauna such as mammoth and giant bison. After these species disappeared, the same wild plants and animals which the later Puebloan people utilized were collected and hunted. The early inhabitants of the Southwest neither produced pottery nor made substantial dwellings. They probably practiced a seasonal round strategy, moving about their territory reusing suitable camp sites perhaps on an annual basis. Late in the pre-Christian period, they may have begun to use a base-camp strategy, where one choice locality was inhabited for a good portion of the year, and people moved out periodically into other areas depending on which foodstuffs were available. The people of the Southwest were not dissimilar to arctic hunters or hunters and gatherers known ethnographically from the South African and Australian deserts.

The first major change in this adaptive pattern occurred sometime between

3 An artist's reconstruction of a typical pithouse of the Late Pithouse period. The hearth lay directly in front of the ramp entrance. The gabled roof, reconstructed on the basis of posthole patterns and fallen timbers from various structures, is still somewhat conjectural.

800 BC and the beginning of the Christian era, when domesticated plants, in particular maize, or corn, reached the Southwest from Mexico. Maize initially seems to have had little impact on the subsistence pattern; it was probably grown as a relatively minor addition to the diet. It may have been planted and then left alone; if conditions were favorable it was harvested in the fall and provided a storable supplement to the diet; if the crop failed, life would have gone on as before and wild plants would have been collected and stored for the winter.

An important and revolutionary change occurred sometime around AD 200. This old nomadic or semi-nomadic strategy was abandoned and permanent settled villages were established. Farming became much more important. Pottery was made for the first time and important modifications in maize-grinding methods also appear. Houses become larger and more substantial. The typical structure was about 5 m in diameter and was dug into the soil about 1 m, hence the name 'pithouse'. A wooden frame was constructed which was then covered with grass and reeds and capped by thick layers of mud or adobe. In the Mimbres area there were lateral entrance ways, also roofed. *fig. 3* Pithouses had the appearance of Eskimo igloos, only they were of earth, not ice. They were spaced apart from each other and villages were simply unpatterned collections of structures, each probably housing an extended family.

Wild foods were still important, but it is suspected that domesticated plants, now including maize, beans, and squash, were important enough to be tended throughout the growing season and that a crop failure would have meant some hardship.

It is at this time – the age of the first permanent villages – that we can first recognize the ancestors of the Mimbres people, and sites of this kind were the most ancient we excavated.

The American Southwest was occupied by a number of prehistoric cultures at different periods, but archaeologists today see three major cultural areas. Interestingly, the regions they occupied correspond well with the major physiographic zones of the Southwest.[5]

The northern area is plateau country, with sandstone mesas (flat-topped rocky outcrops, from the Spanish for 'table') as major physiographic features. The sandstone was used for building, and the great architectural achievements of Chaco Canyon and Mesa Verde were made possible by the quality of masonry available. This northern cultural area is known as the Anasazi, a Navajo word meaning 'Ancient Ones'. Anasazi sites were the first prehistoric ruins to be encountered and studied by early archaeologists, and even today they receive the majority of research effort. Unfortunately, this has led to the assumption that the Anasazi were the major Southwest culture, who spread their traits to adjacent groups. As we shall see, this is not the case.

The second major cultural zone is known as the Hohokam area. These people were generally confined to the low desert country of southern Arizona. Here irrigation was essentially for agriculture. Good building stone was lacking and for most of its history architecture was unspectacular. The Hohokam show many traits with strong Mesoamerican parallels. For hundreds of years they controlled the trade in shell ornaments of various kinds from the Gulf of California.

The final area, the Mogollon, includes the Mimbres people. This region is physiographically the most diverse. Its northern reaches are dominated by rugged mountains with little arable land. South of these are lower foothills, which then give way to what is known as a basin and range area. This consists mainly of flat alluvial fans with occasional eroded mountain remnants. The foothill zone, with streams flowing out of the mountains, proved to be the most habitable and had the largest prehistoric population. The Mimbres cultural zone encompassed a large section of the foothills and the adjacent mountain and basin and range areas. The Mogollon region does not generally have good sandstone and the architecture is less impressive than the more northerly Anasazi. Probably for this reason it was little explored by the early archaeologists. The region's real significance was not realized until the 1930s, so has always been interpreted in the light of its better-known Anasazi neighbor.

Another factor fundamentally affects our understanding of the Mogollon area. In the Anasazi region many prehistoric groups survived into the ethnographic present. These include the Hopi, Tewa, Acoma, and many others. In the Hohokam area also, the Pima and Papago are either descended from or very similarly adapted to the previous prehistoric people. However, no Puebloan people survived in the Mogollon into the ethnographic present, and we have no groups with which to draw close parallels with the prehistoric occupants. The famous Apache who used much of the territory are, like their close Navajo relatives to the north, unrelated to the Puebloan Indians and they are latecomers to the Southwest, probably arriving after the Spaniards first entered the area. Moreover, their adaptation has been very different from the sedentary Puebloan farmers of the past, and so provide a poor analogy with the Mogollon archaeological remains.

The Mogollon cultural area has been divided into several geographical sectors. Each of these has some distinctive traits, but all share enough features for the encompassing term to be useful. For many years all the groups were considered to have developed along parallel and equivalent lines. We must now reject this notion. The Mimbres were the most densely settled, had the largest sites, the most elaborate pottery-painting traditions, and the biggest and most complex ceremonial structures. In these and other ways they differed from their neighbors. Many differences are probably related to the distinct habitat of each group. Much of the Mogollon area is mountainous, which precludes the population densities that were possible in the Mimbres area. Moreover, the open plains to the south of the valley facilitated trade with a variety of groups while bypassing the mountains. As a consequence, the Mimbres were really the innovators in the Mogollon region; most of the rest of the people did not produce painted pottery for many years, but received it in trade from the Mimbres.

The Mimbres had a history different from their mountain neighbors, but they disappeared suddenly from the archaeological record in the 1100s, while the mountain Mogollon survived until much later.

In sum, the Mimbres were participants in a pan-Southwest way of life, which revolved around sedentary village farming. The population of the American Southwest was not homogeneous; major cultural subdivisions existed from early in its history, and the Mimbres appear to have been a major group within one of these.

The setting

The American Southwest has frequently been called Oasis America. It is surrounded on three sides by areas where horticulture was not feasible, as was also the case in certain parts of the Southwest itself. Broad zones totally unsuited to farming are interspersed with small pockets of potentially more productive land.

The Southwest is generally characterized by a semi-arid climate. Moisture is a product of two different weather patterns. In the winter, storm fronts moving from the west coast produce snow and provide about half the annual precipitation. The resultant soil moisture is important in the spring for the germination and early growth of crops. The humidity is low and the sun is very hot, quickly drying out the land. By June the soil moisture is just about depleted. The weather regime shifts in midsummer to a season of thunderstorms. Moisture comes up from the Caribbean, is heated by the sun, and enormous thunderheads are produced. These bring violent thundershowers in the afternoons. These storms are a major problem for the archaeologist, frequently washing us out, but they are critical for the crops.

There are several important implications to this weather regime. First, it is marginal. In a typical year there is just barely enough moisture to grow crops even in the best areas. Relatively small deviations from normal can bring disaster. The second implication is that this rainfall is quite unpredictable and varied. The winter precipitation differs considerably from year to year, with good years having several times as much moisture as bad years. The summer thunderstorms are also unpredictable. They may be only a few miles wide and move along a track for a few hours and then dissipate. Thus one field may get 1 cm of rain in an hour, and a field less than a mile away may get nothing. Precipitation rarely evens out in the short run, so in the same valley some fields may get two or three times more moisture than other fields during a single growing season. As if this were not enough, the Southwest experiences cycles of wetness and dryness. The drought cycles may last 20 to 30 years. Not all years are bad. Nevertheless, during bad periods it is possible to lose two or three crops in a row due to drought conditions. All these factors, of course, had an enormous effect on the aboriginal populations.

First of all the need for rain must have permeated their lives. The historic Pueblo Indian religion is heavily involved in seeking the gods' assistance in providing adequate rain. Water becomes an important image in this dry land, and water-related motifs are frequent on Mimbres bowls. There were other results of the rainfall regime. One was that the Mimbres chose to live along permanent water courses in the optimum zones for growing food. As we shall see, they probably employed irrigation techniques to minimize the effects of vagaries in rainfall.

The quantity of precipitation is heavily influenced by elevation. Mountains force the air higher and the consequent cooling increases rainfall. So the upper reaches of the Mimbres Valley at 2130 m receive twice as much rain as do the open plains at 1375 m.

However, rainfall was not the only limitation imposed on the aboriginal farmers. While the Southwest does not receive a lot of snow, it does get quite cold, and crops must be planted and allowed to ripen between the last frost of spring and the first killing frost of the fall. The length of the growing season, or frost-free period, is very largely dependent on elevation. In general, the higher one goes, the shorter the growing season. In lower desert areas this may average 160 days, while in the mountains it may last only 100 days. At these upper altitudes it is almost impossible to get maize to mature consistently. Thus we see that the very places that have the best rainfall pattern have the shortest growing season, while the arid plains have very long seasons but inadequate water. This is a perfect example of the oasis concept. Between these extremes there are areas which have barely adequate rainfall and a scarcely long-enough growing season; yet these are the best regions for farming.

The environment of the Mimbres Valley

This discussion of the Southwest environment has been rather general, and it is important to look at the Mimbres Valley itself in detail.[6] The headwaters of the Mimbres are characterized by forests of ponderosa pine, douglas fir, and spruce, usually on steeply sloping topography. This zone has the greatest precipitation, averaging 50 cm per annum. The agricultural potential is severely limited by the short growing season, as it lies above 2135 m.

The most important zone in the Mimbres Valley is a pigmy woodland comprising oak, juniper (cedar), and piñon pine. Trees are often no larger than big bushes and are spread far apart. With an average rainfall of 40 cm and a relatively long growing season this area is capable of supporting rainfall farming as well as irrigation agriculture on the broad floodplain of the Mimbres River. The floodplain supported a floral community dominated by cottonwoods. The river is usually quite small and slow and can easily be *plate I* waded or crossed on a fallen log. Periodic floods do occur, and these sweep away trees, bridges, and houses built in the floodplain. Even in this middle stretch of the valley, most of the side drainages entering the river are mountainous and rugged and were never very productive.

The Mimbres River flows out onto a shrub and grass covered floodplain. This desert, lying below 1680 m, has a low rainfall of about 25 cm per annum, although it does have a very long growing season. The low rainfall and high evaporation rate make the area unusually poor for farming, except in a few *plate II* restricted places where surface water-flow permits irrigation agriculture.

Tree-ring dating

One aspect of this semi-arid climate with particular significance for archaeology, involves the growth rings on trees. The conifers and junipers (cedars) of the Southwest almost always add a single ring each year. But due to the wide fluctuation in rainfall from year to year, they add rings of rather different widths. This has enabled the dating of archaeologically recovered pieces of wood (and charcoal) often to the actual year when the tree was felled. This ability to date sites by tree-ring counting has allowed us to establish the highly accurate chronology for which the Southwest is now famous.

The technique was developed in the 1930s by an astronomer, Andrew E. Douglass, with the cooperation of archaeologists. Douglass realized that any fairly long sequence of growth rings would produce a unique pattern, because the rainfall pattern is never identical over say a 30- to 40-year period. He and his colleagues began to establish the chronology by finding large living trees. They knew the date when they cut the tree, and hence the date of the outer ring. With this information they were able to establish the tree-ring pattern *fig. 4* over the last few hundred years. Then, by finding old beams from historic structures, they could extend the chronology back still further in time. This

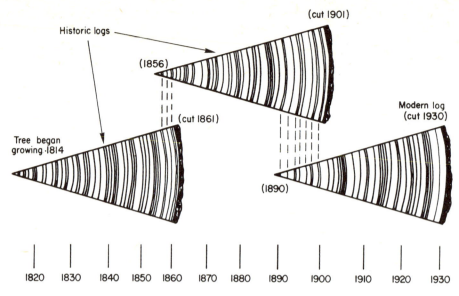

4 *The tree-ring dating method relies on matching the parallel ring patterns from different trees. Here, the innermost rings of a log cut in 1930 are matched with the outermost ones of an older tree. By counting the number of rings of the modern wood we know that it dates from 1890, allowing us to determine that the older tree was cut in 1901. Repeating the same process with the innermost rings of this second tree we can, in turn, date a still older tree that began growing in 1814. This process has been carried back some 2000 years in the Southwest. Other specimens can be matched against this master tree-ring sequence and dated.*

was accomplished by finding a beam whose outer rings matched the growth pattern of the inner rings of the oldest part of the chronology. The inner part of this new piece would extend the chronology back in time. The date of each ring is established by simply counting the number of rings in our sequence. Since we know the date of the outer ring (the year we cut the tree) and since there is one ring each year, we can easily obtain the date of the innermost ring. There are some complicating factors which make the method somewhat more elaborate than this description suggests, but the basic principle remains quite simple.

The Southwest was combed for old beams and trees and quite soon a tree-ring chronology was established from the present back to the AD 1200s. At the same time, archaeologists were busy collecting wood and charcoal from archaeological sites. The specimens were pieced together to form a sequence of tree-rings many hundreds of years long. However, since all the specimens were from ancient sites, none of which could be situated historically, there was no way of establishing the absolute or calendar dates for this sequence. But in the summer of 1929 a particularly exciting breakthrough occurred. A beam was found in a ruin in Arizona which bridged the gap between the earliest rings from the historical period. Its innermost rings matched the latest rings on the archaeological chronology. Instantly the dates could be computed for all the archaeological sites that had produced beams, and over thirty of the major sites were well dated. While this discovery may not have been as spectacular or as widely publicized as the finding of Machu Picchu or of Troy, for example, it was in its own way one of the great archaeological discoveries of our time.

As so often the case in archaeology, what appears simple in theory is not easy in practice. In the Mimbres area, one of the most common prehistorically used woods, juniper, does not add a single ring every year, so it is impossible to obtain dates from these specimens. Moreover, one needs samples that are at least twenty-five or thirty rings wide. In our case many valuable examples were probably spoilt by previous pothunting that had broken the pieces and made them too small to date.

As if these difficulties were not enough, during some time-periods in the Mimbres Valley almost all the wood used to build the roofs was cottonwood, a tree that grows in the river bottom and consequently gets its moisture from the water table and not from rainfall. Its rings are therefore of equal width each year and consequently undatable. Thus although we collected hundreds of pieces of cottonwood, juniper, or broken charcoal from some sites we obtained no dates. Even worse, the vast majority of all archaeological excavations in the Mimbres Valley were carried out before the tree-ring technique was perfected, and all the charcoal was discarded.

Nevertheless, in spite of all these difficulties we have for the first time recovered a wide range of specimens that have been tree-ring dated and which give us precise dates for the Mimbres people.

3 Archaeology and the Mimbres

True archaeological interest in the American Southwest did not really begin until the 1880s. The area had only become American territory some thirty years before and was still lightly settled and generally poorly known. Early research concentrated on the Anasazi zone to the north, and while the Mimbres area was known it was not considered very important. There were several reasons for this. The Anasazi territory was still occupied by Puebloan groups whose relationship to prehistoric sites in the region was clear and interesting. Moreover, Anasazi sites were both spectacular and well preserved. Besides the almost completely intact cliff dwellings such as the Cliff Palace at Mesa Verde, non-cave sites were also still impressive. When Richard Wetherhill opened a trading post at Chaco Canyon he moved his goods inside some rooms at Pueblo Bonito whose walls and roofs were still intact and standing 5 stories high. While no one realized at the time that Pueblo Bonito had been abandoned for over 700 years, it was clearly very old, and it is not surprising that early interest focused on sites such as this.

Nothing comparable existed in Mimbres country. Sites were never more than one storey high. Their walls of river cobbles and adobe have weathered badly and are now under 1 meter high. Windblown sand and melted adobe and rock simply filled the rooms and buried the walls. Today the ruins appear as very low, barely perceptible mounds with a few potsherds and pieces of chipped stone on the surface.

The Indian inhabitants, various Apache groups, were clearly not descendants of the Pueblo people. They were not seen as historically fascinating but as a real threat to life and property, even at this late date. Lack of interest in the fragile architecture of the region was more a reflection of the quality of the archaeology of the day. When Walter Hough conducted excavations just north of the Mimbres area soon after the turn of the century, he found a very large kiva but did not grasp that it had been a roofed building. Instead he described it as an open dance plaza, thereby classifying it as a feature of minor architectural importance.

Although the area was not considered particularly important, it did receive attention from the majority of early experts, including several respected and influential pioneer American archaeologists. Probably the most famous of all these early explorer-archaeologists, Adolph Bandelier, visited the Mimbres Valley in 1883 and noted the presence of many ruins. Shortly thereafter, in

1889, Clement Webster mapped and dug sites in the same area. Walter Hough, from the US National Museum, also visited valley sites and prepared a very early report on the Mimbres pottery. Unfortunately he did not excavate there, but moved further to the north. Even Nels Nelson, often considered the father of American archaeology, visited in 1912 and carefully mapped almost all the major Mimbres sites.[7]

These early archaeologists were surprisingly uninterested in Mimbres pottery. Their reports either do not discuss it at all, or make only casual mention of its color, pattern, and general characteristics. Clearly some of them had seen naturalistic bowls or at least large sherds from such pieces. Then why this lack of interest? The only explanation is that no one saw enough complete, naturalistically painted bowls to realize they were an important aspect of Mimbres art. The vessels were generally found in burials deep below the floors of rooms and most sherds on the surface were broken so small that the naturalistic motifs were unrecognizable. Since these early archaeologists did little or no digging, it is not really surprising that the full significance of Mimbres art went unnoticed for over thirty years.

It was amateur pothunters, especially E. D. Osborn of Deming, New Mexico, who changed our perception of the Mimbres ceramic tradition. Osborn excavated a number of bowls from a site on his ranch and from others in the area. Many vessels bore naturalistic designs, and he sent copies of them to the Smithsonian Institution. Their decoration was so unlike anything known from the Southwest that J. Walter Fewkes visited the area in 1914 and purchased a collection of pots from Osborn for the Museum. Fewkes visited some sites and may even have done some excavation. Additional purchases and visits were made as late as 1923.[8]

During the mid-1920s and early 1930s a major wave of excavations took place in the Mimbres area. These revealed most of what was known prior to the work of the Mimbres Foundation. It was clearly the golden age of Mimbres archaeology. Wesley Bradfield conducted excavations at the Cameron Creek site to the west of the valley, and at Three Circle Village at the headwaters of the river.[9] It seems that Bradfield was making real progress at deciphering the evolution of Mimbres pottery and architecture. His untimely death prevented him from developing these ideas, and the publication on the Cameron Creek excavations is only an abbreviated compilation of his field notes.

At the same period Harriet and Cornelius Cosgrove, who were local residents of nearby Silver City, began a major excavation project at the Swarts ruin in the valley.[10] The Cosgroves had no formal training in archaeology, but spent time working with A. V. Kidder who was excavating at Pecos Pueblo near Santa Fe. On the basis of this experience they spent four seasons excavating the Swarts ruin. Their field notes have survived, and the quality of their recording and digging is quite impressive. They employed procedures that have not become common until quite recently. However, most of this information has remained unused and unrecognized because their report on the project was rather general and incorporated little of the data they recovered.

While the Cosgroves and Bradfield were still in the field, work started on the Galaz site, where the Southwest Museum of Los Angeles had begun a long-term project. They were assisted by the Cosgroves whose son was the crew chief. The field notes from this project have not survived, nor was any major publication ever produced. After only one season, funds apparently ran out and the expedition was recalled. Almost immediately a project from the University of Minnesota took over the site. They first worked with Bradfield to gain experience and then spent three seasons at the Galaz ruin. The Minnesota field notes, which are still available, were quite good for the period; however, no important publication was ever forthcoming.[11] While the Minnesota project was still in the field a two-year excavation program was initiated at the Mattocks ruin, 6 miles upstream from the Galaz site, by the Logan Museum, Beloit College.[12] The quality of their work really did not match that of the other Mimbres projects, but some of the notes have survived and contain useful information.

plate 9

The final important project of this era was that done by Emil Haury. He began by trying to define the eastern limits of the Hohokam culture (see the map in *figure 1*), but when he got to Mimbres country he quickly realized that here was something quite different. He first worked on a pithouse village site at the extreme northwestern corner of the area, called Mogollon Village after a nearby town. This name was also given to the Mogollon culture. He then made the important decision to move to the Harris site in the Mimbres Valley itself, a pithouse village without a later surface Pueblo occupation. From these two excavations he established both the ceramic and architectural sequence and produced the first tree-ring dates for the Mimbres culture. He originated the concept of the Mogollon as a group of cultures distinct from the Anasazi to the north and the Hohokam to the west, and determined both the sequence and the approximate placement in time of some five hundred years of Mimbres history.[13]

The basic framework that was developed from all this work has survived careful scrutiny. It was discovered that pithouse villages existed from about AD 600 to AD 1000, and that afterwards, surface pueblos were built. An evolution in the shape of pithouses was also observed. The basis of the pottery sequence, beginning with plain pottery and developing into the famous black on white bowls, was established at the same time, and collections of other artifact types were recovered which broadly defined the nature of the material culture of the Mimbres.

Although this great flurry of activity in the 20s and 30s did produce a lot of information, bad luck prevented it from reaching its potential. Research on tree-ring dating had only just begun, and chronologies had not yet been worked out. None of the specimens from Cameron Creek, Three Circle,

Swarts, Mattocks or the Galaz sites were saved; a really great loss. One consequence was that the dating of the Pueblo or later part of Mimbres history was left to guesswork, and the guesses were generally not very precise. This inaccurate time-sequence produced theories about the Mimbres people that are now clearly untenable.

Secondly, the only excavation of a Mimbres pueblo which was properly published was the Swarts site, and in some ways this was an atypical one, as we shall see. Only recently has the unpublished information from all these sites been analyzed and used in our interpretation of the Mimbres. Our own research has included a re-analysis of all the Galaz work, and of the Swarts and Cameron Creek field notes. Examining these old records has led to a quantum leap in our understanding of Mimbres burial practices, painted-pottery design evolution, and architectural developments.[14]

After Haury's important work in the mid-1930s, the Mimbres Valley received forty years of benign neglect by archaeologists. An occasional salvage project was mounted because of road construction, and some small excavations or site surveys were performed. Work of a more intensive kind was carried out by James Fitting along the western edge of the Mimbres area in the early 1970s, but few results have ever been published. Such efforts contributed little to our overall understanding of the Mimbres, because no attempt was ever made to synthesize knowledge in the light of new information. In this same period, pothunters continued their destruction unabated. Thus the labors of the 1920s and 1930s will always represent an important body of data on the Mimbres, because so little now remains to be excavated.

When we began work in 1974, we had some of the information from this early period, mainly in the form of the published reports of the Cosgroves and Nesbitt. We were dependent on a conceptual framework that was about forty years old, and our ideas about the origin, development and demise of the Mimbres were primarily a product of that early phase of research. Our work on the Mimbres has to a considerable extent included a 're-excavation' of the field notes and a re-examination of the ideas of the early archaeologists. This was a source of information which we could not ignore. Just as we had to learn how to extract information from potted deposits, we also needed to squeeze all we could out of the previous work, and ferret out the misconceptions that had so long been accepted.

Color plates *(pages 33–36)*

I The Mimbres Valley near the Galaz site. The current farming of the valley bottom can be seen. In the distance is the knoll known locally as Apache Hill. On its summit are the remains of a large village of the Early Pithouse period dating to AD 200–550.

II The Mimbres River flows out of the mountains onto a broad desert plain interspersed with eroded mountain remnants. Favored localities were used by the Mimbres people, but most of the region was uninhabited.

III Turquoise was a very valuable item in the prehistoric Southwest and was widely traded. It is frequently found in the form of pendants, often as two matched pieces perhaps to be used as earrings.

IV The size-range of Mimbres bowls is quite considerable. The large specimen on the right is 25.4 cm in diameter while the center bowl has a diameter of only 14 cm. This small bowl shows two bears. The example on the far left should be compared with that in plate 56, which has two stylized ram heads. This takes the abstraction one step further; only the rams' horns are shown.

V Two figurative Classic Mimbres bowls. The right bowl shows a bat; that on the left a long-necked crane eating a fish, while a small human head floats without any body in the upper left. This is the same iconographic representation as that in plate 74.

VI A series of Mimbres bowls showing contemporary representational and geometric designs. The upper-left bowl shows a humpbacked man – a figure commonly depicted in the Puebloan Southwest. A woman is riding on his hump, wearing a sash and balancing a basket on her head. The bowl on the lower right shows a man with a bear. The bear-tracks and the bow and arrows beside the man suggest that this is a hunting scene.

VII These five bowls show the rare use of tan-colored paint on Mimbres bowls, always used as a filler element. The bowl in the center has only a geometric design at first glance, but in fact depicts two baskets with tan bases.

VIII A series of early Mimbres bowls. The upper left bowl is Mogollon Red on Brown, the first painted Mimbres pottery. It evolved into Three Circle Red on White bowls, two of which are shown to the right. Below are several forms of Boldface Black on White type, which evolved out of the Three Circle Red on White.

I

II

III

IV

V

VI

VII

VIII

4 The beginnings of the Mimbres culture

When we began work in the Mimbres Valley in 1974 we decided first to excavate Mimbres pueblo sites. We knew by now that structures of the preceding Pithouse period existed and we expected to find them there. We also knew that other parts of the Mogollon region contained much earlier pithouse villages, but none had ever been reported in the Mimbres Valley.

Although we had not yet begun our systematic survey, we did a non-systematic reconnaissance of the valley and the immediate environs. An isolated knoll near our field camp offered an excellent view. Although it was a strenuous climb, it was undertaken by a team who came back to report the presence of a site on the knoll.

The McAnally site

The McAnally site, named after the owner of the land on which it was located, *fig. 5* was quickly realized to be much earlier than others we were working on. The presence of plain brown pottery and no painted types suggested that the place had been occupied before other pithouse structures like those at the Harris village. It turned out to date from the Early Pithouse period.[15] The site contained about fifteen pithouses, as evidenced by depressions on the surface. These practically cover the top of the knoll. Pithouses were normally dug into the subsoil a meter or more. When they collapsed after abandonment, the roofs caved in and earth slowly began to fill the hole. Usually this resulted in a shallow dish-shaped depression 3 m or 4 m across, that remains visible on the surface for example at the McAnally site. Typically no subsequent occupation occurred on the Early Pithouse period sites. On later settlements, that were subsequently reoccupied, the refuse produced by the population usually filled the pithouse depressions so that they became completely invisible on the surface.

During the 1974 season time was limited, so only one-half of one of the structures could be examined. We initially mapped the site and numbered the pithouse depressions; the structure chosen for excavation was number 8. This was selected because it was at the center of the site. We reasoned that the first structures were most probably in the center of the knoll and later structures would surround the earlier ones. Thus Pithouse 8 may have been one of the

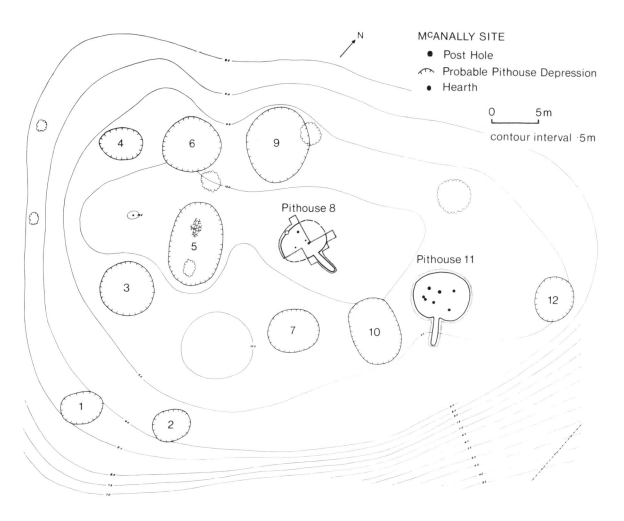

MCANALLY SITE

N

● Post Hole

⌒ Probable Pithouse Depression

● Hearth

0   5m

contour interval ·5m

Pithouse 8

Pithouse 11

4   6   9

5

3   7   10   12

1

2

5 Plan of the McAnally site, an Early Pithouse period village which dates from AD *250–550. Part of Pithouse 8 and all of Pithouse 11 were excavated.*

earlier structures on the site. Since one of our interests was how early the site was first inhabited, this structure seemed a good choice.

We excavated Pithouse 8 by employing what is really an Old World archaeological technique. We presumed that the structure would be circular, as are pithouses of this period elsewhere in the Mogollon area. Because of the presence of the depression on the surface we had a very good idea of where its walls would be. We conceived of the structure as a pie and cut it into four large pieces. We then excavated two opposite pieces. We also knew that the ramp entrance to pithouses usually opens to the southeast, so we adjusted the pieces of our pie to include the area where we expected to find it. As can be seen in figure 5 this strategy proved completely successful.

At that point we thought our luck had run out. In later pithouses the hearth had been found directly in line with the rampway. Hearths are important because they contain material which can be dated, as well as a range of botanical remains. We found a scattering of ash in the appropriate location but did not feel confident this was a hearth. So we expanded our pieces of pie to try and find it elsewhere. Our excavations took on a strange look. These expanded excavations did not yield any other feature that could have been a hearth, suggesting that the ashy area we originally found had in fact been its location. Other excavations in early pithouses have shown that these ephemeral hearths are not unusual. Pithouse 8 had not been burned and seems to have been carefully abandoned leaving few artifacts behind. Because of this, the complete excavation of the structure would not have produced much more information. About half the pithouse was left for the future, when new techniques will perhaps enable archaeologists to extract additional information from it.

There was another very practical reason for excavating only half of the pithouse. The soil was like concrete. Every part of the structure had to be excavated with a railroad pick. Trowels snapped like toothpicks and shovels just bounced off the surface. We are not sure why the fill in these structures became so much more compacted than that on any other site in the valley. The greater age, and hence longer time to compact and consolidate, was obviously one factor. This hard soil is not unique in the Southwest. In a mountainous part of the northern Anasazi area similar pithouses (although not so old) have fill that is so hard that the excavators first loosen the soil with explosives.

Another difficulty was the effort required to get to the site. We first had to cross the Mimbres River on a fallen log. Then hike to the base of the knoll, and finally climb 70 m up a very steep slope. This became a serious problem when we had to carry digging tools, screens, material to cover the excavation trenches when it rained, lunch, and water (about a gallon per person) up to the top. Returning was downhill, but the sherds, chipped stone, and other artifacts needed to be carried as well. Moreover, this was thunderstorm season and fast-moving storms produce a lot of lightning. Working on a high isolated knoll – the highest ground for miles – was particularly dangerous, and when any thunder shower got near the crew had to run down the mountain, only to reclimb it when the shower passed.

Our first season's work at the McAnally site was a useful beginning. We learned about the time period and obtained a sample of artifacts, but did not discover much else about it. We did determine that further excavation was going to be a costly, difficult affair, and we hastily assigned it a low priority.

However, carbon samples from Pithouse 8 produced a radiocarbon date of AD 250 ± 60 (adjusted). This turned out to be one of the earliest known pottery-producing villages in the Southwest, and we decided in 1976 to tackle the site once again. This time we applied a different strategy. We decided there was little to be gained by excavating another structure like Pithouse 8, with its paucity of burned wood for tree-ring dating and scarcity of artifacts. We wanted to find a burned house with an *in situ* assemblage of artifacts. The burning would preserve some of the wooden parts of the structure, and if the fire was accidental many artifacts would have been left in place as people fled.

We selected a variety of pithouse depressions – some small, some large, some near the center of the village, some on the edge – and began to put small test trenches into them. This still involved a considerable effort because of the hardness of the soils, and it took a number of days to excavate one of these trenches. On the third trench we struck lucky. We encountered what was clearly a burned structure. We abandoned our sampling effort and decided to excavate this structure fully, which, like all early pithouses, was circular.

Pithouse 11 had indeed been burned, as was indicated by the test trench, and contained an *in situ* assemblage. Pottery vessels, metates (corn grinding stones), and other artifacts were on the floor. Removing them was another matter. They were so firmly imbedded in the soil that it was hard to excavate them without smashing them. At one point water had to be carried up the hill and poured over the artifacts to loosen the soil so they could be removed. A number of tree-ring samples were recovered from Pithouse 11, but all were unfortunately too small to be datable and again we had to rely on the much less accurate radiocarbon methods. Pithouse 11 dated into the AD 500s. Based on comparisons with other parts of the Southwest we now believe this to be very nearly the end-date for the Early Pithouse period. Pithouse 8 was near the beginning; so the two excavated structures on the site spanned the entire Early Pithouse period, which was most fortunate for us. It is likely that the people who lived in the McAnally site performed many of their daily activities outside the pithouses. We would have liked to open up some living areas between the pithouses to recover information about them. We did not find storage pits or well-developed hearths inside the structures; maybe they were outside. However, the soil was so hard that to have excavated a wide enough area to encounter such features was beyond our resources.

The Thompson site

We did no further work on the McAnally site, but we did not give up on the Early Pithouse period. We decided we would learn most by working on another site of the same period at the other end of the valley. The one we chose, the Thompson site, was also on a high isolated knoll (some 50 m above the river), but was not as inaccessible as the McAnally site. Excavation there enabled us to compare the fauna, flora, and other cultural remains of these two Early Pithouse villages. If, as might have been the case, one end of the valley was occupied earlier than the other, a comparison of the dates from the McAnally and Thompson sites would show it. Or, alternatively, the inhabitants may have been using the upper end of the valley in the summer and the lower, warmer end in the winter. These and other possible land-use patterns could best be examined by using information from the two sites at opposite ends of the valley.

Another important reason for working on the Thompson site was that we had conducted excavations on some later settlements in the near vicinity. Direct comparisons of the pollen and other environmentally related material, as well as certain artifact classes from these sites, would enable us to look for environmental changes at the southern end of the valley.

Our expectations were not fully realized. We began by excavating quarters of two pithouses that had been recognized from the depressions left on the surface. We chose to dig one 'piece of pie' initially from each structure, aligning these excavations in an attempt to include the rampways.

The excavations showed the Thompson site to be markedly different from the McAnally site. The McAnally site was located on the remnant of an old gravel terrace, and although very hard the subsoil was quite deep. The pithouses were deeply cut into the ground, with postholes 50 cm below the floors.

The Thompson site, in contrast, was built on a rocky knoll; the soil was only a few centimeters deep, and the pithouses had been chipped out of the rock itself. They were consequently very shallow and had no postholes or other subfloor pits. The inhabitants lived directly on the rock floors, so occasional artifacts could not be dropped and trampled into the floors for us to recover later. One particularly interesting find clearly demonstrated that the people lived directly on the rock surfaces. We found a mortar hole in one floor with a pestle still in place, making it clear that they ground food on the floor itself.

The inhabitants of the Thompson site did not chip hearths out of the rock floors but built fires directly on the rock. The lack of a depression for the fire meant that there was nowhere for ash and charcoal to collect, so we were unable to recover any materials from the hearths. As later Mimbres hearths had been yielding important information on food and firewood uses, this was a great disappointment.

We did no further excavations on these two structures. Our remaining time at the Thompson site was spent on trial trenches in additional pithouse depressions looking for burned structures. But all was in vain. We did not even find enough charcoal for a radiocarbon date. Chipped stone and some pottery samples were found, but the site simply did not contain the information we were looking for. This work at the Thompson site completed our researches on the Early Pithouse period in the valley. But data we recovered could still be combined with work done elsewhere in the Mogollon region to give us a broad understanding of this important period.

The Early Pithouse period

Most of the prehistory of the Southwest was taken up by what is labeled the Archaic period. Lasting several thousand years, it was a time of hunter-gatherer survival in a semi-arid environment. All topographic zones were used, and we imagine small mobile groups living out a foraging existence. Although maize –ultimately derived from Mexico – was being used, it does not seem to have been very important. Structures were built, at least in some circumstances or seasons, but these were generally small and were shallowly dug into the ground. They were apparently constructed by excavating a slight depression and then planting small poles around the edge and bending them over to form a rounded roof. This framework was then covered with grasses and perhaps mud. No formal entrance way was built, but instead a gap was made, often with a small step, to enter the structure from one side. This form of structure, easily constructed from commonly available materials, was widely used over the world from Paleolithic times to the recent past.

fig. 6   The Archaic people had no pottery. They probably cooked by means of stone boiling, a method which involves dropping hot stones into clay-lined baskets. There were also rock ovens. They did have a maize-grinding technology, consisting of flat slabs or stones with an oval basin and a small round stone termed a basin 'metate', and a one-handed 'mano'. The term 'mano' refers to the stone which is held and 'metate' the stone that is ground upon.

We have no evidence of the bow and arrow at this time. The projectile points we find are large and would probably have been used with a small spear and throwing stick, known as an 'atlatl', the Aztec word for such a weapon. This evidence is substantiated by the fact that dry caves in the Southwest have produced wooden artifacts from the Archaic period, which included parts of spear throwers or small spears, rather than bows and arrows.

Sometime shortly after the beginning of the Christian era, the Archaic people of the Mimbres region came into contact with procedures and with a technology that were capable of revolutionizing their way of life. How they came in possession of these new traits is unclear, except that we are fairly sure it did not involve the movement of new people into the area. Most likely they were acquired from groups in northern Mexico or the Hohokam in southern Arizona.

This new technology consisted basically of a transition to maize farming. It may also have included the rest of the food triad, beans and squash, but it is still unclear when these plants reached the Southwest. It brought with it a new grinding method, consisting of a larger two-handed mano and a metate with a long trough. It appears that the Archaic basin metate and one-handed mano were suited for grinding the small seeds of wild plants in a rotary motion, while the two-handed mano and trough metate were better for the grinding of the larger maize kernels. However, basin metates were still retained although they were relatively rare in post-Archaic sites, and wild seeds continued to be used.

fig. 7   The new technology also included pottery. The first examples are well made and come in a wide variety of shapes. They include both jar and bowl forms.

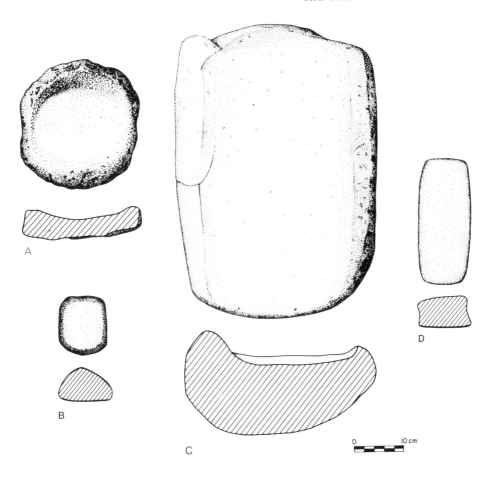

6 *The round basin metate (A) was probably used together with the one-hand mano (B) to grind wild seeds and nuts. The trough metate (C) and a long two-hand mano (D) were more frequently used to grind maize.*

Bowls, which later became very common and the most elaborately decorated form, are relatively rare at this early period. Many of the jar shapes seem reminiscent of gourds, suggesting that the pottery shapes were copies of previously important containers.

The pottery was basically undecorated brownware, although some of it was better burnished and had a reddish hue. Many vessels had a red wash applied to the surface after the pot was fired. This wash was later replaced by a red slip, which was applied and burnished before firing. This pottery ultimately evolved into the Black on White painted ware of later times. The precise details of the ceramic evolution are better viewed from the perspective of the later periods, so will not be discussed in this chapter.

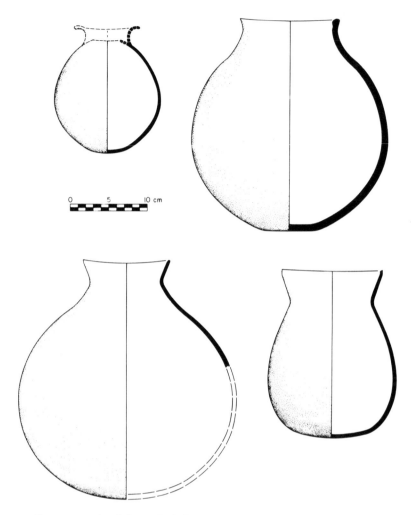

0   5   10 cm

7 Pottery vessels of the Early Pithouse period. These were recovered from Pithouse 11 on the McAnally site and date to the AD 500s.

The most important remaining part of the new technology was an altered building pattern. Structures were now deep (sometimes over 1 m below the original ground surface) and larger (about 15 sq m). They had long ramp entrances. Each change was not great in itself, but their sum total was considerable. The new pithouses required large posts to support heavy earth-covered roofs. The ability to cut these posts apparently depended on the development of the ground stone axe. Although such tools have not been found in Early Pithouse villages in the Mimbres area, they have been found in early village deposits elsewhere in the Mogollon region. It is clear that these structures required a much greater labor investment than did the Archaic houses. One needs only to remember how difficult it was for us to excavate the McAnally site to imagine how hard it must have been to dig the houses in the first place. The amount of energy subsequently required to build the roofs was also substantial. This implies that these structures were more permanent than previous ones. An important consequence of such durable buildings must have been better storage for agricultural products.

The Early Pithouse period, as demonstrated by the McAnally and Thompson sites, seems therefore to have been a time of transition to a more sedentary and agriculturally more dependent life-style. All the developments that followed on were ultimately due to this major change.

The transformation did not occur throughout the Mimbres area. Instead it was concentrated in the well-watered valley. Both the higher mountain zones and the lower, more arid areas were largely abandoned. This does not mean the other areas were not used at all. They certainly must have been. But villages were not established there at this time. The population of the entire region seems to have been concentrated in a few villages in the Mimbres Valley.

We have located some thirty-three villages in the valley which date to this period, and these have on the average seven pithouse depressions each. Since we conducted systematic site surveys over only about a third of the valley we expect there were considerably more villages to be found. The location of the sites is most striking. They are all built on ridge tops or isolated knolls. The Apache Hill site is an extreme example of the positions favored by these people *plate 1* (although the name is wrong as there is no evidence that the Apache ever used the hill). It is some 275 m above the valley floor, where the nearest water source was located. All wood for construction and fires, as well as water, food, and all other supplies had to be carried up this very steep hill.

While other sites were not positioned on such high knolls, they too were on steep, elevated locations and required considerable work just to get up and down each day. This settlement pattern, clearly in evidence in the Mimbres, has been noted elsewhere in the Mogollon area, and a wide variety of explanations have been offered for it. Some have argued that an important food resource was located on these hills, and others that they reflected the ceremonial needs of the community. Yet another reasonable explanation is that isolated hills and ridges were chosen for defensive purposes. At the close of the period these high places were abandoned and never again used as village sites by any inhabitants of the valley.

We currently favor defense as an explanation for the location of these villages, but our uncertainty points out the difficulty in drawing conclusions from archaeological information. We can be sure that living in these places was costly in terms of the work needed to build them and to bring supplies to them. We can also surmise that for the first time quantities of food were being stored in villages, so only the fear, real or surmised, of their loss could have required defensive sites. We also know that at the end of the period the bow *plate 24* and arrow was introduced into the region, perhaps changing the military balance and rendering the hilltops less easily defensible and so explained their abandonment.

45

However, all the evidence is inferential. We have no actual evidence of warfare, no sacking of villages or unburied bodies, nor proof that the bow and arrow rendered the hilltops obsolete. Such evidence is hard to come by, and it may take years of excavation to verify this hypothesis.

The Early Pithouse period lasted from about AD 200 until AD 550. After that date, early sites were abandoned and the population moved to lower ground adjacent to the Mimbres River.

We have every reason to believe that this change of location was not the result of new peoples moving into the valley or due to the arrival of fresh ideas, but was simply a result of the different requirements of the Early Pithouse people themselves. The material culture found in the new settlements is much more clearly recognizable as Mimbres than was that of the Early Pithouse period. As we shall see, this was because of a series of small changes in the material culture and was not part of any radical transformation, such as the displacement of the entire population.

5 The Galaz site

Our work in the Mimbres Valley aimed to cover the whole of prehistory, but we really concentrated on two closely related periods, called by us the Late Pithouse period and the following Classic Mimbres, or Surface Pueblo, period. Since both are almost always found on the same large sites it is difficult to discuss them separately.

Our work at the Mattocks ruin and at the Bradsby, Wheaton-Smith, and Montezuma sites concentrated on the Classic Mimbres period. The Galaz site gave us the opportunity to concentrate on the preceding Late Pithouse period, although, as we shall see, it was an important Classic Mimbres pueblo as well.

The fate of the Galaz site really encapsulates the history of Mimbres archaeology. It is not a pleasant story. The settlement was discovered soon after the turn of the century when pothunters began to dig into it. The village lies on a terrace just above the Mimbres floodplain, at a particularly important location. The valley bottom at this point is especially wide and is farmed today by simple gravity-feed irrigation canals. The modern highway that crosses the valley from west to east passes nearby. This is approximately the same route that Lieutenant Emory traversed when he explored the region after it was acquired by the United States following the war with Mexico of 1846–8. He undoubtedly followed a well-defined trail, as the area was not uninhabited. So it seems that the Galaz site lay at a particularly good location for an east-west trail. It is likely that one existed in prehistoric times as well. Today the town of San Lorenzo, the largest and longest-occupied settlement along the river, lies just over the water from the Galaz site. The Galaz site was probably a particularly important Mimbres village.

During the 1920s an expedition from the Southwest Museum in Los Angeles began work there. After excavating about ten rooms, they ran out of funds and were recalled. Soon after, however, a new expedition from the University of Minnesota, under the direction of Dr Albert E. Jenks, began a four-year project on the site. They excavated numerous Classic Mimbres rooms as well as underlying earlier pithouses, and two major ceremonial structures. This work has never been published, although many years later some MA theses included data from the project.[16] Because no reports appeared, the site was largely forgotten by Southwestern archaeologists.

plates 9, 11

The Galaz site had not been totally excavated by these early archaeologists, and pothunters continued to dig into it. In the 1970s it was leased so that a

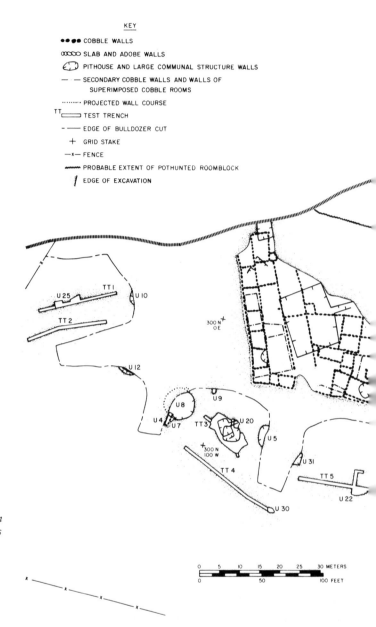

KEY

•• •• COBBLE WALLS

∞∞∞ SLAB AND ADOBE WALLS

PITHOUSE AND LARGE COMMUNAL STRUCTURE WALLS

— — SECONDARY COBBLE WALLS AND WALLS OF
    SUPERIMPOSED COBBLE ROOMS

········ PROJECTED WALL COURSE

TT▭ TEST TRENCH

- — EDGE OF BULLDOZER CUT

+ GRID STAKE

—x— FENCE

PROBABLE EXTENT OF POTHUNTED ROOMBLOCK

EDGE OF EXCAVATION

8 This plan of the Galaz pueblo shows both
the village layout and the history of digging on
the site. The Pithouse and surface room blocks
excavated by three different research projects
are shown. The extent of the bulldozing prior
to our work is also marked.

professional pothunter could completely bulldoze the area to recover the
remaining painted bowls. At that time we were just beginning our work in the
valley and had not yet realized how much could be learned from plundered
Mimbres sites. Although we had known about the Galaz site before the
bulldozing began, we did not grasp its potential and made no attempt to
excavate there.

By 1975, after our second field season, we had learned how much
information we were capable of recovering from such sites. Three-quarters of

RIO MIMBRES

TRUE NORTH   MAGNETIC NORTH

0 N
200 E

EDGE OF FIRST
RIVER TERRACE

100 S
200 E

150 N
100 E

U 17

U 16

U 18

TT 15

200 S
50 E

U 28

TT 14

150 N
0 E

U 14

TT 16

0 N
0 E

TT 18

U 15

TT 13

150 S
0 E

U 27

U 32

TT 11

TT 12

U 42

50 N
00 W

U 3

U 29

U 41

U 40

0 N
100 W

TT 10

TT 19

U 24

TT 6

U 11

U 6 & 13

100 S
100 W

TT 9

U 19

U 23

U 2

U 1

U 21

TT 7

U 26

TT 8

it had now been totally bulldozed. The heavy machines had systematically
gone back and forth across a large portion of the area. At each pass bowls were
exposed and rooms and other deposits were destroyed. All scientific
information and architecture had been completely obliterated. Tony Berlant
went to the site and persuaded the people bulldozing it that they should allow
us to excavate some remaining portions before they were flattened. The men
agreed and after our regular field season ended we began work at the Galaz
site.

fig. 8 Unfortunately it is not easy to begin a new research project at such short notice. Most of the students had to return to their universities at the end of the summer vacations, and the winter was fast approaching. Worst of all, the excavations had not been planned for, and no finance existed for the work. We did what we could. The edge of the bulldozer-cut had revealed an excellent profile, and one could easily see the outlines of pithouse depressions in the section. This, of course, meant that at least part of each structure we could see had already been destroyed. But we could not tell how much was lost and how much remained. By walking the entire length of the bulldozer-cut, which extended over several hundred yards, we recognized a number of pithouses. We tried to work on about eleven of these. Most turned out to be almost totally gone, and the small fragments remaining were of only limited value. We encountered three that were at least half intact. These turned out to be particularly significant, including a very important early ceremonial structure. Our procedures were the opposite of the bulldozer's, since university-trained excavators dug each pithouse individually by levels (15 cm) and screened each one for artifacts. Pollen samples, soil samples, and botanical samples were recovered, as were tens of thousands of potsherds and pieces of chipped stone. Over one hundred complete and fragmentary manos and metates, as well as many other artifacts, were found in their proper archaeological context. These were therefore of scientific value.

The pithouses were covered and filled up with waste material both from the Late Pithouse period and the subsequent Classic Mimbres period. As all the surface Mimbres structures had by this time been bulldozed, this refuse took on particular significance. By careful excavation we were able to recover important information on the ceramics, chipped stone, and faunal and floral remains. This enabled us to compare the Classic Mimbres-period occupation at this site with the preceding Late Pithouse period, and the settlement as a whole with other sites in the valley.

Excavating the refuse increased the time required to excavate each pithouse, and by the time we finished it was cold and the money had run out, so work was stopped for the winter. We returned in the spring with a limited crew. Again, it was not the usual digging season and vacations had not begun, nor did we have adequate funds. We employed a different technique at the site. Using the backhoe of a tractor we made long trenches through parts of the site that had not yet been bulldozed. Under carefully controlled conditions power equipment can be an important archaeological tool and a fully justified one. At the Galaz site, we had no compunction whatever about using the backhoe; we knew the site would be totally bulldozed in a few months and we needed to find the remaining structures as fast as possible.

A number of pithouses were discovered in this way. As we cut shallow trenches each pithouse would show up as a refuse deposit extending below the usual ground surface. The backhoe was then stopped and moved to a new location on the site to search for other pithouses. This work was done carefully

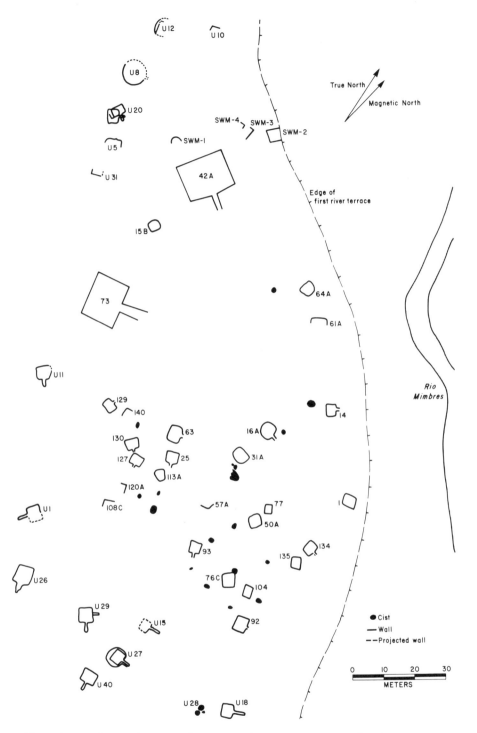

9 *The Galaz site during the Late Pithouse period, AD 550–1000. Not all pithouses were contemporaneous, nor were the two great kivas (42A and 73). Numerous cists, or outdoor underground storage pits, are also shown. Not all the pithouses are shown here, because little of the site was scientifically excavated. There is no overall plan to this village, nor any consistent orientation of the rampways.*

Color plates *(pages 53–56)*

IX Five Classic Mimbres representational bowls. Paired figures are quite common. The spacing of the rabbits and of the insects is typical, while the joining of the turkeys is not.

X Four Mimbres bowls that show the range of colors of this generally black on white pottery. The fantasy animal on the right appears in black paint. The top bowl and that on the left were done in the same material, but different firing conditions resulted in a red and brown color. The bottom bowl, in black, has tan paint used as a filler.

XI Two Classic Mimbres bowls. The one on the left shows a hawk or an eagle with a tan wing, carrying a half-eaten rabbit.

XII Three early Mimbres bowls. Above is a Three Circle Red on White bowl made in the AD 700s. Below are early Boldface Black on White bowls of the AD 800s. They were excavated from the Galaz site by the Mimbres Foundation.

XIII A Classic Mimbres bowl showing a moth resting on a sword or wand. Such wands are sometimes depicted as tall as a man, as in plate 78, or as a rabbit in plate 71. The Mimbres made a wooden staff several feet long of this kind, as in plate 32.

XIV The historic Pueblo Indians of the Southwest twirled a small wooden object called a bullroarer on a long string, producing a buzzing sound. This Classic period bowl probably depicts such an activity. The bullroarer appears very large in comparison to the man, but this may be an attempt at perspective, with the bullroarer in the foreground.

XV A small Classic Mimbres bowl showing a human figure wearing a necklace.

IX

X

XI
XII

XIII

XIV

XV

so that no deposits actually associated with the pithouses themselves were touched, only the overlying refuse layer.

Nine of the best-preserved pithouses, including two types that had never been identified before in the Mimbres area, were excavated before our allotted time on site ran out. Unfortunately, other structures had to be left unexamined. The day following our departure, the bulldozer went back to work and the remainder of the Galaz site was quickly destroyed.

We had uncovered several burned features in the pithouses at the Galaz site, including adobe-covered walls and adobe hearths. These would have allowed the technique of archaeomagnetic dating to be used, as we had successfully done on other sites in the valley. A sample of the baked earth can be taken, and the magnetic north in existence when it was fired compared with the contemporary situation. This is a complex but highly accurate dating method. Unfortunately, no one on our crew was trained in the technique of taking the requisite samples. There were few experts in the Southwest, and we were unable to get one to the site before it was finally bulldozed. We later learned that a very large ceremonial structure, dug in the 1920s, had not yet been completely bulldozed. We might have been able to redig it and recover materials for dating had we known of its existence in time.

The following year, when Katherine White was photographing the collection of Mimbres bowls from the Galaz site at the University of Minnesota for the Mimbres Archive, she found that the complete set of original field notes existed. We were able to copy these, and have learned a great deal about the site from them. Since this early work was done before the days of tree-ring dating and other modern techniques, the excavators recovered little environmental or subsistence information. They did, however, get a very large quantity of architectural and artifactual data. This was a perfect complement to our own work at the site. We recovered quantities of environmental and subsistence information but only a relatively small number of pithouse structures and no Classic Mimbres surface rooms. A thorough re-analysis of all the Galaz material has been completed by Roger Anyon and a final report is being prepared.

We now know that the site was founded around AD 600 or a little before. Fortunately, one of the buildings we excavated – the ceremonial structure Pithouse 8 – was one of the earliest in the settlement and dated to the early 600s. Across the river from the Galaz on a high ridge was an Early Pithouse village. This site, now mostly obliterated, probably housed a community which subsequently built the Galaz site, since this was founded just after the settlement-pattern shift away from the high ridges to the valley itself. In all likelihood the people living on the Galaz site in the 1100s were descendants of an occupation in the immediate area from about AD 200 onward, first on the ridge across the river and then at the site itself.

The early excavators were not able to date the pithouses they excavated at the Galaz site, but we now know that the earliest pithouses were round like their predecessors, and that later ones were square or rectangular. Thus we can roughly date the pithouses excavated by the University of Minnesota. As the site was never completely dug we can only estimate the number of structures built at any one period.

fig. 9   It appears that the site began as a small village of about fifteen pithouses, at least one of which was a ceremonial structure. Later the number increased until by the end of the Late Pithouse period it contained about forty-five domestic structures, and at least two more, much larger ceremonial structures. The pithouse village at its maximum extent covered an area roughly 100 m by 260 m, and perhaps held as many as 200 inhabitants.[17]

The Late Pithouse period we now know lasted from about AD 550 to about 1000. During this time the population grew substantially, and most of the major villages were established. As we shall see, there were important developments in domestic architecture, ceremonial structures, and in the pottery tradition.

6 Architectural developments at the Galaz site

Our work at the Galaz site substantially filled out our knowledge of both domestic and ceremonial architectural developments for the Late Pithouse period, especially when combined with the University of Minnesota excavations. The pattern of development coincides with that found at a number of Mimbres sites, including those in the valley that were excavated by us.

The basic framework was developed by Emil Haury who worked in the valley in 1934. But we now see the Mimbres sequence as divided into three broad periods, the Early Pithouse period from AD 200 to 550; the Late Pithouse period from 550 to 1000; and the Surface Pueblo or Classic Mimbres period from 1000 to 1130. Ours was the first research on the Early Pithouse period in the valley. Sites were on hilltops, pithouses were round, and the pottery was plain. Sites of the Late Pithouse and Classic Mimbres periods were both located on terraces adjacent to the river bottoms, and usually the same site was occupied by both. This resulted in pithouses frequently being overlain by the cobble-walled surface rooms.

Researchers who preceded Haury concentrated on the surface pueblos of the Classic Mimbres period, and in the process found underlying depressions of the Late Pithouse period. Haury decided to work on the earlier period exclusively and worked out a three-part temporal division for its 450 years. He named these the Georgetown, San Francisco, and Three Circle phases, on the basis of architectural and ceramic types. Haury probably succeeded where others had failed because he made the important decision to work on one of the few Late Pithouse villages that was not occupied into the Classic Mimbres period. At the Harris site he avoided the confusing effects of these later deposits and was able to concentrate on just the Late Pithouse period. Although a number of archaeologists had recently preceded him in the area, none had deciphered the pithouse sequence. Not only was his work at the Harris site an important step forward at the time, but his conclusions have withstood the test of almost fifty years of subsequent archaeology and are still the best framework for this period of Mimbres prehistory.

Haury gave the name Georgetown to the first part of what we now call the Late Pithouse period because of a nearby historic ghost town. In the 1930s there was very little evidence for the length of this phase, but we now know it lasted about one hundred years, from AD 550 to 650. Two major diagnostic aspects of this period were round pithouses and the lack of painted pottery, just as for the preceding Early Pithouse. Despite some architectural and ceramic differences, the continuity between these two periods is very strong and clear. The change in settlement location from hilltops to the first terrace just above the river bottom, however, distinguishes them. The most interesting other new development was the building of substantial ceremonial structures. We were fortunate in discovering important examples of pithouses and ceremonial structures from this phase at the Galaz site

Domestic architecture

We excavated both a domestic and a ceremonial structure dating to the Georgetown phase. The domestic structure, Pithouse 20, was round with a typical ramp entrance. It had subsequently been built on top of and into by a later house and so was not fully intact. It was similar to other structures of the period. These structures often have a large center post and other smaller ones. In other cases several equally large roof posts are present. It is very difficult to determine how these and later pithouses were roofed. It has been suggested that early examples had conical roofs and that later ones were flat. However, there is evidence that at least some later structures had gables. The question of roof construction, although interesting in its own right, is important for another reason. If roofs were flat, then they could have served as work areas. Many domestic functions could have taken place there as well as, or instead of, inside.

No roof-top assemblages have been recovered from excavated structures of this early period, and it is likely that roofs were not flat and were not used as living areas. The domestic structures of the Georgetown period were not burnt and had been systematically cleaned out before abandonment. Few artifacts were left behind. This was not the case with the ceremonial structures to be examined below. The Georgetown domestic pithouses had very simple hearths, but these were an advance on the Early Pithouse period practice of building fires directly on the floor. There were still no internal divisions in these houses, no bins, storage rooms, or other structural subdivisions. Burials continued to be situated away from the structures.

After about AD 650 architectural developments at the Galaz site became far more interesting, and our work has filled out our knowledge of both domestic and ceremonial architecture for the remaining part of the Late Pithouse period, from 650 to 1000. What is really striking is the broad continuity of domestic architecture from around AD 200 until the arrival of above-ground architecture some 800 years later. Mimbres architecture underwent a gradual evolution, without rapid transformations.

From our modern perspective, the change to surface architecture seems so sensible that one wonders why it took eight centuries to happen. However, under certain conditions there may be no inherent advantage to surface architecture. Semi-subterranean pithouses were very well suited to the environment of the Southwest. At first, the digging of pits without metal tools may appear an impossible effort. But if sticks were used to loosen and remove rocks and soil immediately after every rain, the task would have been greatly eased. If the operation were spread out over the entire summer rainy season, it would probably have involved much less work than we may think. In addition, pithouses did not require much wood, a relatively scarce commodity in the Southwest and difficult to prepare with the Mimbres' technology. The resulting structures probably had greater thermal efficiency than surface rooms. They were half dug into the ground and had a thick coating of earth over their upper parts. Such insulation was important not only for the cold winters, but also would have protected against the heat of the summer sun. We suspect that a small hole was left in the roof to let smoke escape. Fresh air would have flowed in through the long ramp entrance and then up the smokehole. The small hearths, always situated in front of the rampways, show that large fires were not needed to heat the houses. We need to consider rather why these structures were given up, not why it took so long to convert to above-ground masonry houses.

During the later part of the Late Pithouse period, there were further changes in domestic architecture that probably accompanied a new roofing pattern. The period also saw an elaboration of interior features, most notably hearths. More frequent remodeling of structures is in evidence, and one finds the first use of masonry walls, an important precursor to above-ground masonry structures after AD 1000. Of all these changes, the most obvious and the most significant involved the shape of the pithouses. Early pithouses were round; the style then became basically rectangular, but with rounded sides and corners; and the latest ones were fully rectangular or square. These changes occurred individually, each representing a relatively minor change.

The pithouses at the Galaz site provide a good understanding of the architectural developments. Pithouse 27 was really two structures, each presenting an archaeologically complex but revealing situation. Excavations first revealed a rectangular pithouse with a ramp entrance. Further digging showed that an earlier round pithouse had existed at this spot. Unfortunately, the rectangular pithouse so closely overlaid the round one that little of the earlier structure remained. *fig. 10, plate 17*

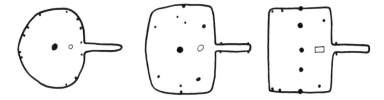

10 Three stages in the evolution of pithouse architecture. Early structures were circular or bean-shaped. Later pithouses were rectangular with rounded sides. The latest pithouses were rectangular or square.

The round one, with its ramp entrance, had been used for an undetermined length of time. It was abandoned and a rectangular pithouse was built in the same location with the rampway slightly offset, although it retained the same orientation. The floor of the new pithouse was at essentially the same depth as that of the earlier structure.

This evidence suggests what the sequence of events may have been. If the round pithouse had fallen into disuse for any length of time, the roof would have collapsed and the walls crumbled, and the pit would then have been partially filled. If this were so, it is very unlikely that the subsequent rectangular pithouse would have been built perfectly within the round structure, at exactly the same depth, and with the rampway similarly oriented. Everything points to there having been little delay between the abandonment of the round structure and the setting up of the rectangular one.

Could this new building simply show that the owners were keeping up with changing fashion? Did the round pithouse become out of date and the rectangular style popular? Maybe the round pithouse was dismantled and rebuilt to conform to this new style. An alternative explanation also exists. Pithouses seem to have had limited life-spans. Either the roofs and beams eventually became old and rotten, or perhaps vermin reached unacceptable levels. Houses typically underwent occasional remodeling during the latter part of the Pithouse and Classic periods. This may have happened to the round structure. Maybe the style had changed between the building of the pithouse plate 15 and its reconstruction, so that the remodeling incorporated the new shape.

Pithouse 29 also showed evidence for remodeling, but of a different kind. It was originally a square structure with the rampway pointing northeast and a round hearth in front of its opening. Two series of events followed which may or may not have been related. The first was the abandonment of the rampway and hearth. A wall was built across the ramp where it entered the room and the hearth was covered over. A new cut was made in the southeast wall and a rampway and new hearth made. We are able to link these changes to tree-ring dates. The ramp relocation must have necessitated changing or adding some fig. 11 roof timbers, although most of the beams were retained. For this reason we found a cluster of tree-ring dates from the burned roof of around AD 859 and a second one of around 870. The first group probably dates the building of the pithouse and the second the relocating of the rampway.

Some time before the pithouse was remodeled, however, a burial pit was made in the corner of the room and ten infants buried in it. They were not interred in a regular pattern, but the burials did not disturb each other, suggesting that they were all contemporaneous or nearly so. Before the abandonment of the pithouse, a number of rabbit skulls were placed in the hearth. It was never used again as these were not burned; the pithouse was then deliberately burned.

One can speculate on reasons for these events and their order. The most likely sequence is that the pithouse was built in AD 859. A number of infants

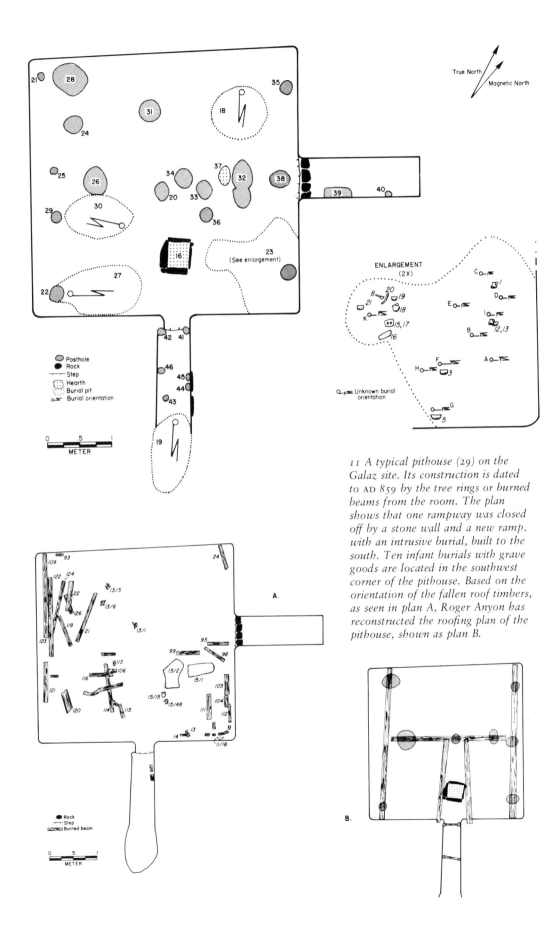

Posthole
Rock
Step
Hearth
Burial pit
Burial orientation

ENLARGEMENT
(2X)

Unknown burial orientation

True North
Magnetic North

0   .5   1
METER

11 *A typical pithouse (29) on the Galaz site. Its construction is dated to AD 859 by the tree rings or burned beams from the room. The plan shows that one rampway was closed off by a stone wall and a new ramp, with an intrusive burial, built to the south. Ten infant burials with grave goods are located in the southwest corner of the pithouse. Based on the orientation of the fallen roof timbers, as seen in plan A, Roger Anyon has reconstructed the roofing plan of the pithouse, shown as plan B.*

A.

Rock
Step
Burned beam

0   5   1
METER

B.

later died and were buried under the floor. Their closeness in age precludes them from being of the same family. Perhaps some epidemic hit the village and they were interred together. Later, perhaps because some other building was in the way, the location of the rampway was no longer desirable. It was relocated in AD 870. Finally the rabbit skulls were placed in the hearth and the pithouse was burned. Were the rabbit skulls a final offering to the infants when the structure was abandoned? Such speculation is intriguing, but we are unable to provide any answers.

An even more enigmatic complex of structures was excavated at the north end of the Galaz site. A rectangular pithouse with rounded sides had first been excavated into the ground. This structure, Pithouse 20, was subsequently abandoned and the depression began to fill up with debris. Sometime later a new structure was built partially on top of the old one. We were unfortunately unable to tree-ring date either of these. The new structure was dug into previously undisturbed subsoil as well as into the fill of the original abandoned pithouse.

The new building differed from any previous Mogollon structure. The rectangular room had walls of large cobbles set in adobe, but it was still semi-subterranean. Architecturally it represents a transition between pithouses dug into the soil whose walls were simply of earth plastered with a coat of adobe mud, and rooms on the surface with walls built of large cobbles. At least half the walls and the whole roof were visible above ground. It was similar to a pithouse in that it was semi-subterranean and was detached or isolated from any other structures. It was structurally close to later cobble-walled surface rooms, but the setting was different, since these were almost invariably combined into blocks. So in a number of ways it was transitional between the major architectural forms.

fig. 12 Cobble architecture was used in another semi-subterranean structure at this site – one of the great kivas. A more common early use of cobble was for building stone walls to shore up weak sections of otherwise typical pithouses. This need most often arose when a pithouse was excavated into soil that had previously been dug into. The soft fill was not as structurally sound as the original undisturbed subsoil of the first terrace. In such instances cobble walls seem to have been a way of preventing collapse. This may be an explanation

plate 14 for the later cobblestone pithouse in Unit 20. That rectangular structure was dug partly into the earlier round pithouse. Cobble walls would have been needed inside the newly dug hole to keep the loose fill from sliding in.

Thus, what started as a solution to the problem of collapse soon became a more general architectural technique, and we must remember that these pithouses were only partially underground, so the tops of the cobble walls would have been exposed for up to 1 m above the surface. This would have necessitated a new technique of roof construction. But as soon as this had been mastered, one had all the technology necessary to build a cobble-walled surface room. The builder simply copied Unit 20 but did not dig a hole first.

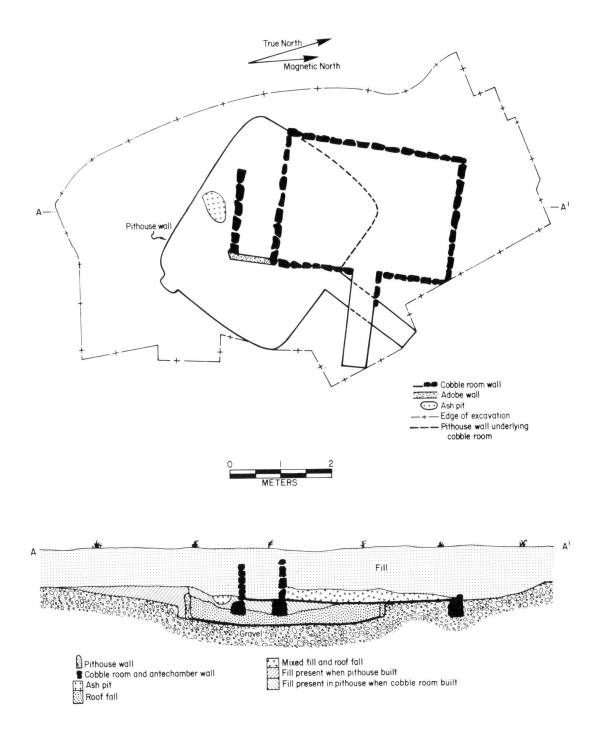

True North

Magnetic North

Pithouse wall

- ▬●●● Cobble room wall
- ▨▨▨ Adobe wall
- ⬭ Ash pit
- ─+─ Edge of excavation
- ─ ─ ─ Pithouse wall underlying cobble room

0   1   2
METERS

A   A'

Fill

Gravel

- ◉ Pithouse wall
- ⬛ Cobble room and antechamber wall
- ⬚ Ash pit
- ⬚ Roof fall
- ⬚ Mixed fill and roof fall
- ▨ Fill present when pithouse built
- ▨ Fill present in pithouse when cobble room built

12 *Two superimposed structures from the Galaz site – an early pithouse and a later cobble-walled subterranean room. The pithouse was built around* AD *650–750, and the later cobble room added just before* AD *1000, at the time of transition from subterranean pithouses to surface rooms. It was built partially below ground, but in the construction techniques of later surface rooms.*

While this certainly does not explain why the Mimbres decided to build surface rooms, it does make clear how they were in a position to do so once the decision was reached.

Ceremonial architecture

Up to this point we have seen how domestic pithouse architecture evolved. But there were developments in ceremonial architecture as well. Its origins lay in the Early Pithouse period, before A D 500. It reached a climax just before 1000. The evolution of ceremonial or 'great kiva' architecture was first outlined by Haury in the 1930s. But it wasn't until we began to study the original Galaz field notes from the Minnesota Expedition that the full extent of this tradition was grasped.

The work undertaken by Roger Anyon of the Mimbres Foundation has clearly demonstrated how scientific knowledge accumulates.[18] Published data existed for about half the known kivas in the Mimbres area. The other half were recorded in notes and manuscripts on file at museums in the Southwest. The vast majority of these documents had been available for over thirty years, and a good deal of the field work was done over forty years ago. Yet no one had tried to synthesize the information. Roger Anyon began by compiling and ordering all known data on the Mimbres area kivas. By doing this he discovered a pattern that made sense not only of the Galaz kivas (which were his main concern) but of the evolution of Mimbres great kivas in general. He showed how the development of Mimbres kivas closely parallels that of great kivas in other areas of the Mogollon.

fig. 13   In the simplest terms, Mimbres kivas were archaic or anachronistic forms of domestic pithouses on a greatly enlarged scale. Their architectural development consistently lagged behind that of domestic building. When they finally

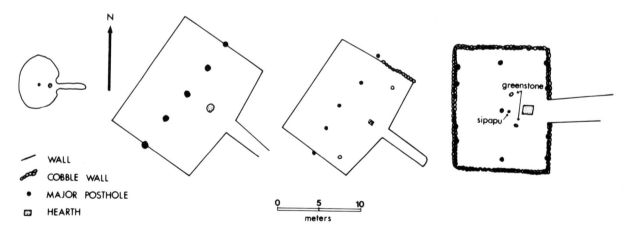

WALL
COBBLE WALL
• MAJOR POSTHOLE
▨ HEARTH

greenstone
sipapu

0   5   10
meters

13 Plans of great kivas from several periods, with a typical round domestic structure for comparison.

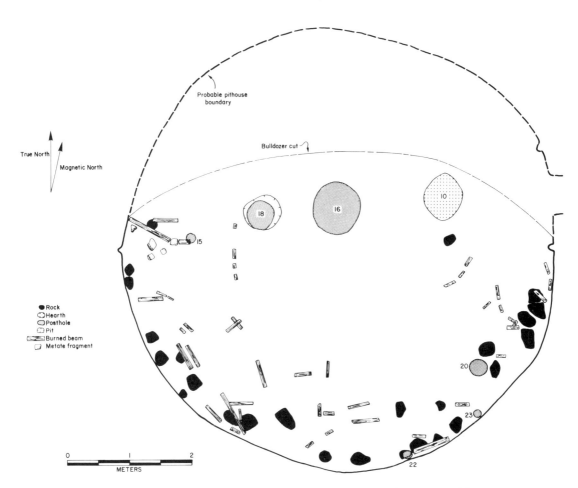

True North

Magnetic North

Probable pithouse
boundary

Bulldozer cut

10

18

16

15

● Rock
◓ Hearth
◔ Posthole
◔ Pit
▭ Burned beam
▱ Metate fragment

20

23

22

0   1   2
MMMMMM
METERS

14 The plan of Great Kiva 8 on the Galaz site. This structure was partially destroyed by a bulldozer. Dating to the AD 600s, *it is one of the earliest kivas in the Mimbres area. Around the edge of the floor were large flat rocks, probably used as seats.*

caught up with innovations in pithouse dwellings, the great kiva was abandoned as a structural type.

The earliest great kiva on the Galaz site was Pithouse 8. This was an example of a very early Mimbres ceremonial structure, dating to the AD 600s. When we examined the profile made by the bulldozer on the site, we were able to see clearly where the pithouse had been dug into the subsoil, but we could not determine how much of the structure remained. During excavation we realized that the bulldozer had already destroyed almost exactly half of the pithouse, including all the entrance rampway.

The structure was round, about 7 m in diameter, and had a floor of about 37 sq m. Our estimate of the initial population of the village was about sixty people, and we think it likely that the entire population of the Galaz site could have attended ceremonies held in this structure.

fig. 14

We believe Pithouse 8 was a ceremonial structure, or great kiva, and not a dwelling, for a variety of reasons. One argument, of course, was its large size; it had approximately two and a half times the floor area of typical domestic pithouses of that time. Moreover, although the pithouse burned in a very hot fire, no domestic artifacts such as metates, bowls, or bone tools were found on its floor. There was, however, a series of large flat stones about 30 cm from the wall. We suspect that these served as seats, or as the bases of seats, and were used by some of the spectators of the ceremonies taking place there. This structure had another feature that suggested its ceremonial function. For a long time, Mimbres ceremonial structures had had some form of architectural elaboration on either side of the ramp entrance. Sometimes these were posts, and sometimes they were earthen pillars or lobes, as I shall discuss below. Pithouse 8 had a stylized lobe, made of adobe, adjacent to where the rampway had been. The heat of the burning had fired the adobe into a hardened ceramic material, so it was well preserved.

Unfortunately, the wooden parts of this kiva had been built almost entirely out of cottonwood, and this riverine species is undatable by the tree-ring method. However, a radiocarbon date of AD 600 was obtained, making this structure probably the oldest known great kiva in the Mogollon region. There are ceremonial structures in other areas that pre-date Pithouse 8, but these also contain domestic artifacts, so may have been dual-purpose structures. Pithouse 8 therefore represents the earliest use of specialized ceremonial structures in the Mimbres area.

Our excavations on the McAnally site uncovered one of these earlier transitional structures, so now we can trace the development of great kivas from their dual purpose predecessors. On earlier hilltop locations, like the McAnally site, we find a few pithouses that are slightly larger than the average domestic structures there. They usually contain a complement of domestic artifacts (when *in situ* assemblages are encountered), including manos, metates, cooking jars, and bone awls. They also possess an architectural feature which is later strongly associated with ceremonial architecture and which was mentioned in the context of Galaz Pithouse 8.

The architectural feature particularly associated with these ceremonial structures consists of elaborating the edge of the pithouse where the ramp enters the structure. In domestic buildings the rampway enters the curved or straight wall of the pithouse as a simple break or opening in the wall. The earliest ceremonial or proto-ceremonial structures have a lobe of earth that projects into the room on either side of the rampway. These lobes extended about 0.5 m and often gave the pithouse the shape of a bean or kidney. We do not know how high these lobes were or what they may have been topped with. plate 16 They soon became more stylized. In Pithouse 8 on the Galaz site, a single lobe survived on the side of the ramp that remained. It was molded out of adobe plaster, was some 10 cm wide, and projected only 7 cm into the room. It extended as high as the wall itself was preserved, 45 cm. Later structures may lack the lobe entirely, but have instead a pair of posts flanking the rampway. Sometimes these posts were placed in postholes; on other occasions they were set on large flat stones.

Once the evolution of lobes or pillars beside the rampway is understood, it becomes logical to expect that early pithouses possessing these features were probably also for ceremonial use. Thus Pithouse 11 at the McAnally site with its domestic artifact assemblage and earthen lobes probably represents a stage at which secular and ceremonial structures were not fully differentiated, some buildings serving both roles.

Ceremonial structures built later than Pithouse 8 at the Galaz site continued to be circular. They also grew in size as the villages expanded, and a typical kiva of between AD 650 and 750 had a floor area of about 63 sq m. The earthen lobes were generally replaced by wooden pillars set on stone slabs. By the end of the Late Pithouse period, great kivas had finally become square or rectangular. Five of these structures have been excavated in the Mimbres area. The two found at the Galaz site are the largest and most elaborate and each warrants a brief description.

Kiva 42A was the largest of all the Mimbres great kivas. It had a floor area of over 175 sq m. The roof was supported by five main roof posts. The center post was set in a hole about 0.75 m in diameter and 2.3 m below the floor. This post rested on three superimposed flat rocks set in the bottom of the posthole.

The interior walls and floor were plastered with adobe between 10 and 15 cm thick. The rampway was about 4.5 m long. Although this was not the largest great kiva ever built – a few at Chaco Canyon are larger – it appears to be one of the five or ten largest such structures in the entire Southwest.

Unlike the small hearths found in domestic structures, Kiva 42A had a square hearth 1 m square. A 'sipapu', a hole placed in the floor in line with the rampway and hearth, known ethnographically as a symbolic entrance to the underworld, occurs in many prehistoric Southwest kivas. This kiva had five sipapus, well plastered and filled with fine white sand.

Kiva 42A was deliberately burned. We suspect it was destroyed to make way   *fig. 15* for a new kiva, known as the Parrot Kiva or Structure 73. This was smaller than its predecessor, but was much more elaborately constructed. A new building technique for kivas was used, setting the scene for above-ground architecture. Instead of walls of earth covered with plaster, the builders used double, wide courses of river cobbles, in which sixty-three support posts were   *plate 10* embedded. The cobble walls and support posts were then completely covered by a layer of plaster.

A hearth, similar to that in Kiva 42A was found, but upon excavation it was discovered to include a sequence of sixteen alternating ash and adobe layers. The final uppermost ash layer was apparently in use when the kiva was abandoned. Only a single sipapu was found in this structure.

A variety of grooves and other features were found in the floor. Perhaps the most interesting were two large polished and shaped greenstones set into the

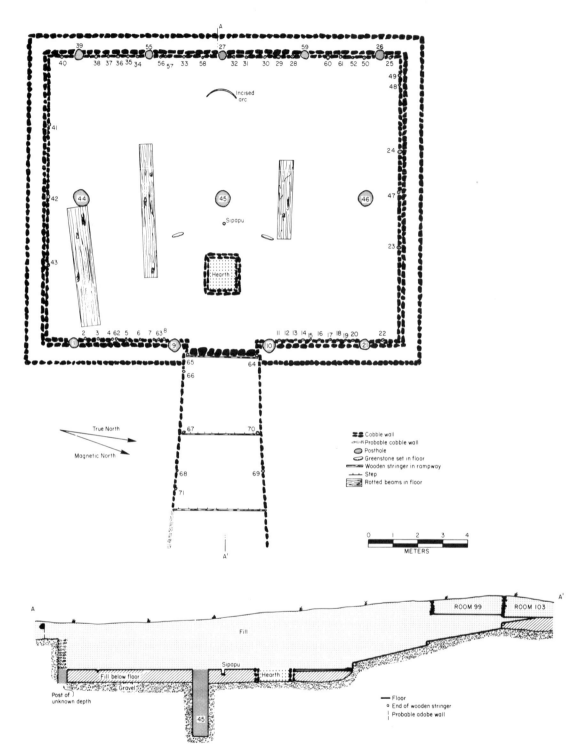

15 *Great Kiva 73 on the Galaz site, excavated by the University of Minnesota. It has double-coursed cobble walls in which were imbedded sixty-three support posts. The roof was held by three major posts. A sipapu, or symbolic hole to the underworld, was found between the hearth and the center post. The structure was about eight times as large as an average house.*

floor. Beneath one of these stones was the skeleton of a parrot which had been interred in strings of turquoise beads. This kiva was abandoned while the pueblo was still occupied, but was not intentionally burned.

These two kivas represent the zenith of kiva development in the Mimbres area, and were the culmination of a fairly regular evolution. Kivas increased in size over time and generally correlate with the size of the village itself. Thus it would appear that kivas were public buildings used by the entire population of a settlement, or at least some broadly drawn sub-population, such as all adult males. They do not seem to be restricted to only a small group or elite unit of society. There was a clear and significant tendency to associate a conservative form of architecture with the kivas, since they remained round when domestic pithouses became rectangular. About 100 or 200 years afterwards, kivas also became rectangular, catching up with the prevalent form of domestic architecture. The only exception to the above pattern is Kiva 42A, which was larger than its successor, the Parrot Kiva. We do not believe that the population at the Galaz site declined at this time. In fact, we expect it to have been expanding. Could this have been the beginning of the decline of great kivas as ceremonial structures which involved the whole community?

No great kivas were constructed on the Galaz site or anywhere else in the Mimbres area during the Classic Mimbres period. When above-ground architecture was first used in the Classic period, great kivas ceased to be built and earlier ones were soon abandoned and fell into disrepair. Ceremonial architecture did not disappear, but was radically transformed, as we shall see. Unfortunately it will be difficult to learn much more about Mimbres great kivas, because only three or four more seem to have survived the bulldozers.

7 The Late Pithouse period

Apart from new developments in the field of architecture during the Late Pithouse period, there were important changes in other areas of Mimbres life. Few of these are more significant than those which took place in the production of ceramics. The 450 years of this period saw the evolution of Classic Mimbres bowl painting. New forms were also appearing in the unpainted utility wares, resulting in the almost complete transformation of this other part of the Mimbres ceramic complex.

The evolution of the painted ceramics is now understood in considerable detail. It really consists of two separate processes. The first is the elaboration of the color pattern itself, and the second is the growth of the design style. The latter subject will be discussed in chapter 10.

The beginning of the Late Pithouse period (the Georgetown phase) saw the development of an important new pottery type. Although it was not painted, it was the forerunner of the entire painted sequence.[19] This was called San Francisco Red, and was made in both bowl and jar shapes, but the bowls eventually predominated. The ware was very highly polished and bright red in color. The outsides of the bowls were textured with dimples, probably made with the thumb before the clay was completely hard. The most important technical feature of this pottery is that the vessels were covered with a thick clay slip to which red hematite had been added to produce the red color. This innovation set the stage for the later development of painted pottery.

The Early Pithouse people had also made a reddish pottery, but this lacked the high polish, the thick slip, and the deep red color of San Francisco Red vessels. The new pottery was therefore less a new arrival than a refinement of the previous redware. The pottery ultimately evolved into the famous Classic Mimbres Black on White pottery which frequently served as a mortuary offering. San Francisco Red also seems occasionally to have been put in tombs. Bowls of this ware are found in the earliest burials that contain ceramics as grave offerings, and the custom of placing well-made bowls in burials as mortuary furniture began at an early stage.

After about AD 650, changes began to occur more rapidly in the Mimbres area. The period until 1000 showed a rapid development of ceramics, architecture, and burial practices. A crucial innovation was the production of
plate VIII
the first painted pottery. Called Mogollon Red on Brown, it evolved simply and directly out of San Francisco Red pottery. All vessels were made in the

form of bowls, just like those in San Francisco Red ware, with the exteriors coated in a red slip and finger dimpled. The interiors were slipped with a clay to which no red hematite was added, resulting in a brown surface. The red slip previously used on the interior was then applied in red designs on the brown background. Thus only a very small change in technique produced this painted pottery. Designs were simple and geometric with essentially no curvilinear elements.

These bowls were not very common. Some were used as grave goods in burials, which at this time were placed in pits away from occupied structures. The soft fill of previously abandoned pithouses was a favorite location. Few burials contained grave goods of any kind. When vessels were interred they were usually placed beside the body, but a few vessels were deliberately broken and the pieces placed in the grave pit. This ritual 'killing' of vessels became more elaborate and formalized as time went on.

The pottery continued to evolve rapidly. Mogollon Red on Brown pottery was produced for about fifty to a hundred years. Then a new color change was made. Instead of using a brown slip, a white kaolin clay slip was applied to the interior of the bowl. This pottery is called Three Circle Red on White. The exteriors were still red slipped, but the finger dimpling had been dropped. The red paint used on Mogollon Red on Brown vessels was also used to paint the designs on the white clay. Also for the first time, painted jars were produced and curvilinear elements began to be used, especially spirals or scrolls. This color change from Red on Brown to Red on White ware took place sometime around AD 700. It could be argued that the objective was to increase the contrast between the background and painted design. The designs on Three Circle Red on White vessels stand out far better than those on Mogollon Red on Brown vessels.

Three Circle Red on White was short lived, lasting at best for a generation or two. Sometime around AD 750 a final color-pattern change occurred. By some means we do not yet fully understand, the Mimbres began to fire their pottery so that the paint became black instead of red. They also stopped using a red slip on the exterior and instead simply smoothed over the clay body. Black paint continued to be applied to a white background for almost 400 more years. The designs used in this new pottery type, Mimbres Boldface, began to evolve rapidly and in diverse ways, but these developments are best viewed from the perspective of the later Classic Mimbres pottery. The predominant Boldface vessel form was the bowl, but very occasionally jars were also painted.

plates XII, 42–3, 45–8

plates 39–40

During the Late Pithouse period another important ceramic innovation took place. Up to this time cooking and utility pieces were plain, with perhaps an occasional punctated or incised piece. Coinciding with the development of the first black on white (Boldface) pottery, the Mimbres people began to decorate their originally plain utility ware and also started to employ some new vessel shapes.

73

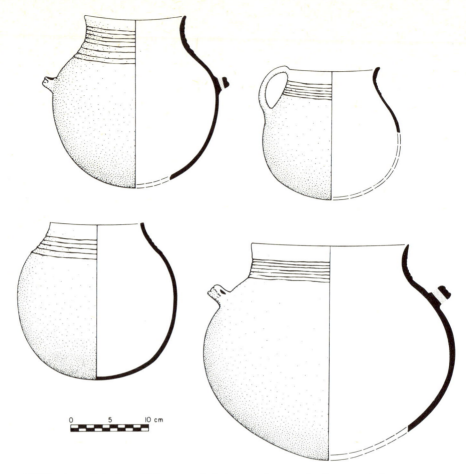

16 Utility jars of the Late Pithouse period show an increase in size over their predecessors and the first use of corrugations. In this period the corrugations are restricted to the neck of the vessel.

The first new decoration consisted of broad bands of clay on the rim and neck of jars. These jars were small and often had braided or strap handles. They look like pitchers and may well have functioned as serving vessels or maybe for drinking a liquid, most likely a form of gruel or stew. Modern Pueblo Indians make pottery vessels by preparing ropes of clay and then coiling them into shape. Then they smooth the surfaces by pressing and scraping. The bands on the necks of these prehistoric Mimbres jars were simply the original coils of clay but not completely scraped down.

The shape of these neck bands quickly evolved. First the bands became much thinner until they were only 4 or 5 mm wide. They are referred to as corrugations by archaeologists in the Southwest. Then they began to use the unflattened coils or corrugations over more of the vessel. Because each corrugation overlapped the one below it, looking like a wall of overlapping horizontal planks or 'clapboards', the term 'clapboard corrugation' is applied

plates 35–37

fig. 16

to this decorative technique. At the same time that these corrugations became common, the Mimbres people began to increase the size of the jars. Thus, as the vessels got bigger, more of their surface was covered with corrugations. By about AD 1000 the entire top-half of the jars were covered with clapboard corrugations and the jars stood some 30 to 40 cm high.

These jars were probably used for serving, cooking, and storage of both food and water. We do not know whether the corrugations served some important function or whether they were purely for decoration. Again, this corrugation was not confined to the Mimbres, but developed in parallel but not identical ways over much of the Southwest.

By the end of the Late Pithouse period the Mimbres had a ceramic assemblage that consisted of painted hemispherical bowls, infrequent painted jars, corrugated jars of several sizes, and very occasionally corrugated or undecorated bowls.

The Mimbres people during the Late Pithouse period

Our excavations threw light on much more than Mimbres architecture and ceramics. Changes in the environment and new aspects of population dynamics are discussed later in the context of the Classic Mimbres period, but we can mention some broad conclusions about the Late Pithouse period peoples here.

By AD 800, at least fourteen major villages had been established in the Mimbres Valley proper, with several minor ones on side canyons leading into it. This, of course, was not the total area occupied by the Mimbres people and large settlements existed elsewhere, especially to the west. However, population density was nowhere greater than in the Mimbres Valley. Most of these large villages were located along the major waterways and in optimal farming areas. At the end of the Late Pithouse period a few small villages began to appear in more marginal locations, such as higher in the pine-forest areas where the growing season is very short. Our current best guess for the total population of the valley at this time is about 1200 people. The total Mimbres people was unlikely to have included more than triple this number.

The Mimbres Valley villages were spaced about every 3 miles along the river. Only one other village may have been as large as the Galaz site, and the remainder were somewhat smaller. Early maps of these largely destroyed sites show that most villages had one or more great kivas at this time. There was little formal planning, and kivas do not seem to have been central structures. Pithouses were not regularly spaced or aligned and ramp entrances did not invariably open to the southeast.

Pithouses were all similar. There were no specialized structures except for the ceremonial ones, and no pithouses used just for storage or food processing. In all likelihood, the nuclear family with perhaps a few additional relatives was the basic economic unit. There is no evidence for political organization at a level above that of the village itself. The villages were built without fortifications and there is no sign of warfare within the valley. Moreover, the similarity between houses and great kivas at these sites, as well as the uniformity of painted designs on the bowls, argues for considerable interaction between communities. Given the small size of many of these villages, there was probably also intermarriage between them. But despite the trade and the marriage, each was probably essentially autonomous. Such a level of social organization is similar to that found among many of the Puebloan villages in the Southwest at the time of the first Spanish contacts.

plate III
plate 27

There was not a great deal of wealth, but what there was seems to have been fairly evenly distributed. Valuable items that survive include turquoise beads and pendants, other stone beads, shell beads and bracelets, stone 'palettes', parrots (which were imported from Mexico and kept probably for ceremonial purposes), and painted bowls. Utilitarian items which required a large labor investment were the metates and ground stone axes. While trade was important, imported goods did not include any which were critical for survival. All seem to have been luxury items.

plate 44

As we have seen, great kivas were elaborate, important structures and must have consumed considerable energy. Religion must have been an integral part of everyday life, but we have little direct evidence for it besides the kivas themselves. Burial practices continued to evolve from the earlier periods. For the first time, we see graves beneath the floors of pithouses that were still being occupied. But a large number of burials took place in other locations. Graves were small unprepared pits, with the body invariably flexed. Grave goods were common but never really abundant, and ceramics were nearly always the most common grave goods. For a while, the deceased were accompanied by a single painted bowl and a corrugated pitcher, but by the end of the period a single painted bowl was the most likely grave offering. For most of the period, ceramic vessels were placed beside the body, or deliberately broken and scattered over the grave. By the end of the period, a small hole was punched in the bottom of a painted bowl, and this was then placed inverted over the head of the deceased. This ritual 'killing' of the bowl seems to have evolved out of the earlier practice of smashing the bowl and scattering the pieces over the grave.

Hunting and farming practices evolved in subtle ways from the earlier periods. Rabbits and deer remained the meat staples, while maize, beans, and squash continued to be the primary crops. There is a surprising lack of storage facilities for these products, unlike the subsequent Classic period.

During the preceding Early Pithouse period, there was sparse evidence for trade with outside groups. Long-distance commerce underwent a great expansion during the Late Pithouse period, and it was at this time that the Mimbres people showed the greatest degree of interaction with adjacent groups. The strongest and most interesting contacts were with the Hohokam of southern Arizona.[20] These had developed into a rather complex society in comparison to others in the region. By A D 700, large pithouse villages had been established in the low desert. These communities were sustained by irrigation agriculture using canals several miles long. Ceremonialism was significantly different from the rest of the Southwest. Low platform mounds and ball courts were the dominant ceremonial-public architectural forms. In place of the general Southwestern pattern of inhumation of the dead, the Hohokam practiced cremation. In addition, a number of Hohokam artifact forms, for example incense burners, are unknown in the rest of the Southwest. These and other reasons have led to the speculation that the Hohokam represented a population that originated in Mesoamerica and migrated to the Southwest.

Regardless of their origins, the Hohokam had a considerable effect on the stylistic development of Mimbres art. This was probably brought about by the movement of traders between the two regions, and not by any significant population movement. We commonly find shell artifacts in Mimbres sites. These quite clearly have come via the Hohokam area. However, other perishable goods perhaps made up the majority of trade items. These may have included cotton textiles. Surprisingly, almost no ceramic vessels were imported into the Mimbres area, although a few Mimbres pieces are regularly found in Hohokam sites. The distance from the Mimbres Valley to the center of the Hohokam area was about 220 miles, and there are no significant physiographic barriers between them, so communication was in fact quite easy. In addition to the shells, two other classes of artifact demonstrate the extent of this trade. Perhaps the most important was the effect on Mimbres pottery designs.

Beginning sometime around A D 800 the Hohokam had a major influence on Mimbres ceramics,[21] whose geometric designs show some close similarities with their Hohokam contemporaries. Also, the Mimbres begin to produce an elliptical bowl similar to a modern gravy boat. This shape was rare in the Mimbres but much more common in the Hohokam area.

plate 41

The most important innovation seems to have been that the Hohokam set the tone for what we now see as uniquely Mimbres art. This involved the use of naturalistic or figurative motifs on the bowls. Three very common Hohokam motifs were a horned lizard shown from above; a bird with its head turned to one side; and a stick-like human figure. These are some of the earliest Mimbres figurative motifs and often appear in the development of Mimbres naturalistic painting. There can be little doubt that these figures were inspired to some extent by contemporary Hohokam bowl painting. This tradition happened to develop into a great art form only among the Mimbres people, while it practically died out in Hohokam painting. The development of sophisticated Mimbres art was a local phenomenon, but based on a borrowed technique.

plates 55, 57

Also important for the Mimbres were the stone palettes. Again, these clearly derived from the Hohokam who had a long tradition which went back to c. A D 300. It was around 800 that Mimbres palettes were first used. They were common only for a brief time in the Late Pithouse period. Never quite as

plate 33

elaborate as those of the Hohokam, and made of local materials, here again this is a situation where the design of the artifact was directly copied, if not the entire concept. But the Mimbres palettes were not simply imitations of imported items. One of the most elaborate of all Mimbres palettes was discovered at the Galaz site. It was found in a cache, beneath the floor of a room that had been built over Kiva 42A after it had been abandoned. The carved feet of the palette are unlike any other Mimbres artifact, and do not match any Hohokam palette either. Where the inspiration came from is not clear.

The function of these palettes has never been determined. Many found at the Galaz site were burial offerings, but this is not the case at other Mimbres sites. Elsewhere, broken fragments are frequently recovered, suggesting that the palettes had a utilitarian function and were occasionally broken and discarded. Traces of paint pigments have been found on a number. Occasionally striations have been noted, suggesting that something had been ground on them. They have been variously considered to be bead-grinding stones, or paint palettes. The Hohokam definitely used them in ceremonies, especially cremations. It is entirely possible that they had many uses, both secular and sacred. These palettes ceased to be used early in the Classic period.

The trade with the Hohokam flourished for about one or two centuries and then greatly diminished for reasons completely unknown. Trade with no other group ever had such a profound effect on the Mimbres. They seem to have traded ceramics and other durable goods for perishable items with many other peoples around them. Most groups did not produce their own painted ceramics at this time, so the Mimbres bowls must have been an exotic and valued commodity. Small quantities are found in all the neighboring areas, but this trade seems to have had little impact on any of their populations.

We can see then that trade does not appear to have been crucial to the development of Mimbres art, although it underwent a brief period of influence from the Hohokam. Trade had little impact during the pre-Classic era.

Up to about AD 1000 the Mimbres population was relatively small. They lived in small autonomous farming villages with unspectacular architecture and an interesting but not unique ceramic tradition. They were not heavily influenced by outsiders nor did they have a major impact on their neighbors. After the major reshaping of their society in about AD 200, change was gradual and internal. The events in the next 150 years gave the Mimbres their place in history.

8 The Classic Mimbres occupation at the Mattocks site

The Classic Mimbres period represented the peak of Mimbres culture. *fig. 17* Villages grew in size and number, and the art tradition reached new heights of skill and sophistication. It was a brief period, lasting only from about AD 1000 to 1150 – less than 150 years. At that point it abruptly ended and the Mimbres people disappeared as a cultural entity. Ironically, although more research has been done on sites of this period than on those of any other in the Mimbres area, its course has been poorly understood. Until recently a number of serious misconceptions about its length, how it ended, and the settlement system have been generally believed.[22]

Sites of this period yield the unique painted pottery which has resulted in the destruction of villages by looters. When we reached the valley in 1974, there were no Classic pueblos which had not been looted. This made our task much more difficult. Archaeologists often compare their research to detective work.

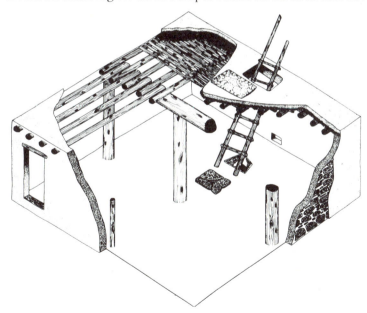

17 An artist's reconstruction of a room from a Classic Mimbres pueblo, dated to about AD 1090. The three-post roof support was typical. An air vent brought fresh air to the room and hearths. One hearth has been covered over with stone slabs. Note the stone for closing the roof entrance.

In the case of the Classic Mimbres, it took a considerable effort just to identify a site which might provide the kind of information we needed. We finally decided that the Mattocks ruin was in better condition than had been imagined. As a consequence, our work on the Classic period focused on the Mattocks ruin, although we conducted excavations on six other Classic Mimbres sites.[23]

The Mattocks ruin lies on the Mimbres River about 6 miles upstream from the Galaz site. As at Galaz, the floodplain adjacent to the Mattocks site is broad and well suited for agriculture. The village lies above the floodplain, at the edge of the terrace about 10 m higher than the river.

plates 12–13

Like most large Classic Mimbres pueblos, the Mattocks site was occupied during the preceding Late Pithouse period. There is reason to believe that the occupants of the McAnally site on the knoll across the river were the founders of the Mattocks community. The area around the Mattocks site was first occupied c. AD 250, while the first structures on the site itself were built c. 550. As the village was not abandoned until c. 1150 there was a settlement here for about 900 years.

The history of excavations at the Mattocks site is all too typical for villages in the Mimbres area. The place was known to archaeologists by at least 1912. Paul Nesbitt, who was with the Logan Museum of Beloit College, brought a small number of students to work there in 1929. It had previously been looted by pothunters. Nevertheless, Nesbitt located and excavated some fifty rooms during his two field sessions. Only a portion of the field notes have survived, and are unfortunately not nearly as good as those taken by contemporary archaeologists working at other sites in the area. Nesbitt also produced a

fig. 18

rather abstract and inaccurate map, which was subsequently to cause considerable confusion when we tried to use it to locate the areas where he had excavated.

Following Nesbitt's work, which was published in 1931,[24] the site was intermittently looted with the consent of the owner. He apparently rented out the right to dig it for a few dollars a day, on condition that the holes were filled in at the end of each day's work. New diggers, therefore, had little idea of what areas had previously been dug, and would reexcavate previously looted ground. Working all day only to discover that a room had previously been dug by other pothunters must have been discouraging. The Mattocks site was never a popular place to dig, and this procedure probably helped to preserve it.

When we arrived there in 1974, some commercial looters had just been evicted, and it was clear that most of the obvious room blocks had been previously dug. We finally realized, however, that the site still had the potential for yielding important information, and we employed an excavation strategy far different from that usually used in modern archaeology.

Instead of sampling the site in an orderly way, we tried to use our knowledge of pothunting techniques to locate rooms which had not been looted. We also used Nesbitt's map to avoid areas he had excavated.

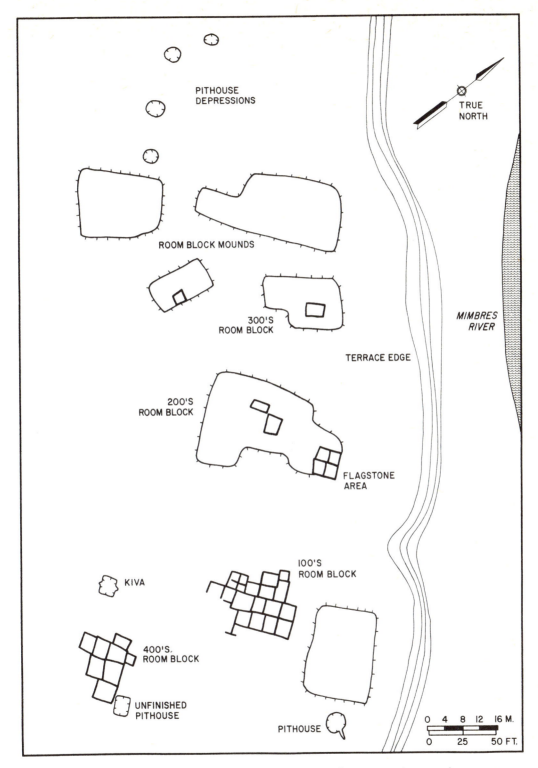

PITHOUSE
DEPRESSIONS

TRUE
NORTH

ROOM BLOCK MOUNDS

MIMBRES
RIVER

300'S
ROOM BLOCK

TERRACE EDGE

200'S
ROOM BLOCK

FLAGSTONE
AREA

100'S
ROOM BLOCK

KIVA

400'S.
ROOM BLOCK

UNFINISHED
PITHOUSE

PITHOUSE

0 4 8 12 16 M.

0   25   50 FT.

*18 A simplified map of the Mattocks ruin. Only a portion of our excavations are shown
and none of the earlier ones. The general size and spacing of the room blocks can be seen,
as well as the possible plaza area between the 100s and 200s room blocks.*

This strategy met with mixed success. In several areas we discovered that Nesbitt had successfully found all the rooms in a block. Since his site map was inaccurate we discovered this only in the course of excavating the structures. In these cases much of our effort was futile, but our time was never completely wasted. Nesbitt had worked before tree-ring dating. Consequently he did not save any charcoal. He apparently threw it back into the rooms when he refilled them. We were able to recover a number of tree-ring specimens from these previously dug rooms, which were very important in dating the Classic Mimbres period.

In order to help us identify rooms and their relationship to each other, we assigned a different series of numbers to those in each room block. Our excavations began on a block to which we assigned numbers starting in the 100s. The second room block we encountered received numbers starting with 200, and so on. Even though we excavated a room numbered '438' in the fourth block, it should be understood that there were never that many rooms on the site. In the following discussion I shall refer to the room blocks as the 100s block, the 200s block, and so on.

In one portion of the 100s block we discovered a group of rooms that had not previously been disturbed, and we were able to excavate a complete row that yielded excellent information. At one end of the row we excavated Room

plate 19

111 which had a hearth and adjacent ash pit; next to the hearth was a large cooking jar. Manos and other artifacts lay scattered on the floor. This was one of the few apparently undisturbed Classic Mimbres rooms where we found artifacts still in place. Most had been cleaned out before abandonment. This row of rooms ultimately produced the crucial tree-ring dates for the Classic Mimbres period, which are critical to our understanding of when the Mimbres disappeared.

We subsequently discovered that much of this room block had in fact been disturbed, showing how mistaken we could be, but encountered an outside work area which was intact. This may have been roofed by a 'ramada', a flat roof used for shade but open-sided like a porch. This did not have a hearth or walls, but a variety of tools and vessels had been left on the ground. We ultimately found other such ramada areas elsewhere on the site. These generally faced south or southeast and provided good shade during the hot summer. They would have been exposed to the sun during the colder parts of the year. We suspect that much day-to-day activity took place under these shelters and not in the rooms themselves.

We thought it likely that some important features of the site would not appear as low mounds as did the larger room blocks. We devised a procedure to look for them. Small test pits were excavated in areas we suspected of having structures or other features. Most of these did not reveal anything, or when they did the structure had been previously disturbed.

In one case we dug some test pits into a slight rise which we suspected might have been a room block. When these test pits encountered the sterile subsoil we quickly abandoned the area. The following season Patricia Gilman, who was the site supervisor at the Mattocks site, had second thoughts. She decided we had abandoned the area too soon, and she began to dig another test trench a few meters away from the first one. Within a short time it was clear that the new trench had been placed inside a room which had never been identified.

That season we excavated three contiguous rooms. We worked on this room block, which became known as the 400s, during two additional seasons and ultimately excavated a total of eight rooms, an outside ramada area, an unfinished pithouse, and a nearby ceremonial room. In the process we discovered some forty-six burials and forty Mimbres bowls, several of which turned out to be important in our further understanding of the Mimbres bowl-painting tradition. The 400s room block represents the first complete Mimbres room block excavated with modern techniques, and has provided considerable insight into the Classic Mimbres period.

fig. 19

Our work on these rooms was more difficult than expected, when one considers the depth of the rooms. The cobble and adobe walls of a Mimbres room are usually only one stone wide and are often irregularly coursed. When first built, these walls probably stood over 1.75 m high, but they subsequently collapsed; many are now no more than 30 to 50 cm high. The rocks from the collapsed portions of the walls fell into the rooms, and the entire room block was covered by windblown sand and sheet wash.

plates 18, 20

In excavating a room the archaeologist first uncovers a jumble of rock; it is no simple matter to decide which stone is part of a wall still in place and which has fallen from a wall. Consequently, finding the exact line of walls is not easy. If we cleared the soil matrix from around the rocks themselves, the wall would then collapse. So it is often difficult to uncover a wall fully without destroying it. Even after the walls are found and the fallen parts removed, they are hard to record properly and photograph because one has to leave the soil matrix in place to support the cobbles.

Once the walls have been exposed, finding and cleaning the floors is quite easy, but when this is finished, another excavation problem arises. In some places, as many as twelve burials were recovered from beneath the floor of a single room in the Mattocks site. By the time even half of these have been uncovered, there are so many open pits in the floor of the room that there is almost no room left to walk. Excavation technique then includes the art of finding a place to put one's feet.

We are now able to reconstruct the history of the 400s room block and to see how it was organized. It never exceeded ten rooms and did not border a plaza, so it was not the largest or most important one on the site. This is an advantage to the archaeologist because the 400s can probably give us a better understanding of the nature of a typical room block.

Like most Mimbres room blocks, the 400s began small and grew by accretion. An original core of three rooms lay a few meters from a pithouse which was never completed. The family that was building the pithouse may

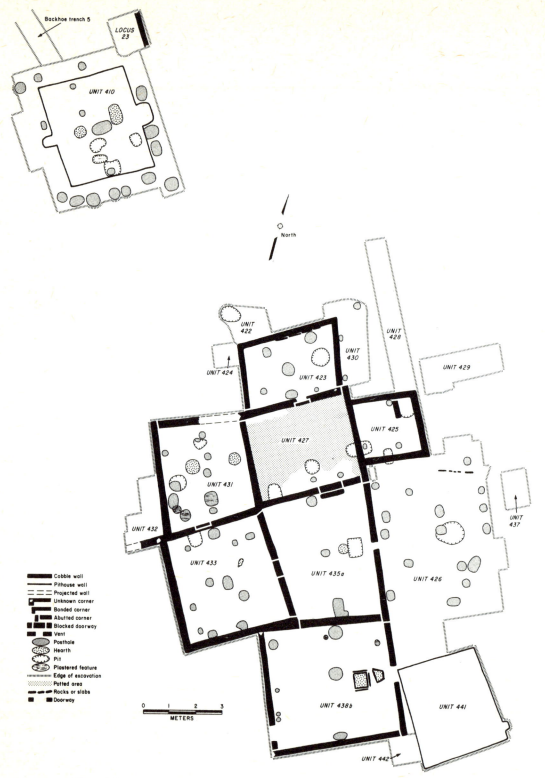

Backhoe trench 5

LOCUS 23

UNIT 410

North

UNIT 422

UNIT 428

UNIT 424

UNIT 423

UNIT 430

UNIT 429

UNIT 427

UNIT 425

UNIT 431

UNIT 432

UNIT 437

UNIT 433

UNIT 435a

UNIT 426

Cobble wall
Pithouse wall
Projected wall
Unknown corner
Bonded corner
Abutted corner
Blocked doorway
Vent
Posthole
Hearth
Pit
Plastered feature
Edge of excavation
Potted area
Rocks or slabs
Doorway

0   1   2   3
METERS

UNIT 438b

UNIT 441

UNIT 442

19 Plan of the 400s room block on the Mattocks site. Unit 441 was an unfinished pithouse, Unit 426 was an outside ramada, and Unit 410 was a pithouse converted into a ceremonial room or kiva.

have decided instead to build these three contiguous surface rooms. The initial occupants probably numbered between five and eight people, a single family.

Sometime later, probably within a generation, additions were made on both sides of the room block. To the south one room and a ramada were added. We know that the room was built in AD 1079. The ramada was soon converted into another regular room. Both were large and had three major roof-support posts. They also had what was either a two-chambered hearth or a hearth with an adjacent warming oven. Air vents brought outside air to the fires. These were clearly habitation rooms where a variety of activities took place.

To the north of the original three rooms a different kind of addition was made. Two small rooms were built. One was clearly a storage room. Only a single small support post was needed for the roof. Instead of a hard-packed adobe floor, like those of the living rooms, it was cobbled, with small stones closely fitted together. This possibly prevented rodents from digging up into the room from below and damaging the stored foodstuffs. The cobbles may also have kept stored foods above any moisture that seeped into the room.

plate 22

The differences between the rooms on the north and on south sides of the room block point to an important new development in Mimbres architecture – the separation of living and storage areas. During the earlier Pithouse periods no such specialization of structures existed. Both storage and daily activities must have occurred within the same undivided area. The subsequent division of space in the Classic period may have served several functions. Storage within specialized rooms would probably have been more efficient, with greater available wall space, and the benefit of specially protective floors. There may also have been a sociological function to the separation of areas. Storage in a one-room pithouse was essentially public; any visitor could see exactly what you owned. In a dual-room system, a visitor to your living room would have been unable to see what you had in your store.

At this stage in its history the 400s room block contained seven rooms. Soon a new ramada was built on the south side. Its floor was found to contain food-grinding metates and the remains of utilitarian pottery. Although most Mimbres room blocks appear to be haphazard in arrangement, the 400s was extended according to an overall plan. Storage rooms were placed on the north side, exposed to the cold winds of winter, while the activity rooms and especially the ramadas were situated so as to be sheltered from the winter winds and to face the winter sun. This arrangement probably assured that as much activity as possible could be carried on outside. Not only would congestion have been reduced in the small rooms, but the light would have been better out of doors.

A final phase of building activity saw the addition of still another living room on the south edge of the block, completing the entire group. We surmise that by the time of this addition some of the original rooms had fallen into disuse, so that the room block probably never had more than seven usable rooms. Besides the surface rooms, a nearby pithouse was converted into a kiva which was probably used by the people of the 400s. Tree-ring dates from the block show that all building took place during the AD 1000s, but we did not recover enough data to place each individual room precisely.

We recovered a total of forty-six burials from beneath the floors of the 400s. They were found beneath the floors of dwellings only, and not of storage rooms. Some dwellings were used more frequently for burials than others, and one room had eleven burials. However, not all of the burials from a room were necessarily beneath the floor of the room itself. Several rooms were first ramada areas or lay just beyond the room block itself. Some interments seem to have been made in these areas, and rooms later constructed over them. Burials were also placed in rooms that had been abandoned.

At first glance, forty-six burials from such a small area seems quite remarkable. If we estimate that the room block was occupied on the average by about 16 people, who on average lived 30 years, and if the room block was used over a space of about 80 to 100 years, we would expect to find from about 42 to 53 burials, which is very close to what we discovered. The best model for the 400s was that it was occupied by a large extended family over several generations, and at any one time had on the average three to four living rooms, two storage rooms, a ramada, and a kiva for this group to use.

Our test pits nearby revealed additional rooms and features, each increasing our understanding of the Mattocks site. We also excavated several long trenches through the areas between the room blocks. We expected to find burials, ramadas, pithouses, and storage pits. In some places this was the case, but between the two largest room blocks on the site we found surprisingly little. We now believe that this was because the space between these two blocks was deliberately kept open and served as a plaza area for public religious ceremonies.

A trench which extended up to the edge of the 200s room block produced evidence which supports this interpretation. Close to the edge of the room block we encountered not a room but a flagstone area. As we excavated, it became clear that this was quite large (20.4 sq m), was unroofed, and was surrounded by a low wall only 30 cm high. The flagstone surface was devoid of domestic artifacts, and was immediately adjacent to the 200s room block on one side and the plaza area on the other. This information leads us to believe that the area may have served some ceremonially related function. Broadly similar but not identical areas are used in such famous historic Pueblo ceremonies as the Snake Dance of the Hopi.

We can now describe the history of the Mattocks site with reasonable accuracy. Our excavations show that it began as a pithouse village at some time around AD 550 to 600. As at the Galaz site, the earliest pithouses were round. These were replaced by square or rectangular structures. Sometime around AD 1000 pithouses were no longer used for habitation, and surface rooms began to be built. We found no evidence of an architectural transitional stage between pithouse and surface rooms at the Mattocks site as we had done at the Galaz site. This may indicate the speed of the transition.

plate 21

As mentioned above, one of the pithouses near the 400s room block had never been completed. The hole for the structure had been dug, but neither roof posts nor the roof itself had ever been erected. The depression had been rapidly filled in and the area then used to build surface rooms. This was not the only example of this sequence of events encountered in the valley. At the Mitchell site we also found a pithouse that had been abandoned before completion, filled in, and built over by surface rooms.

A second pithouse encountered at the Mattocks site had a slightly different history. Pithouse 115B was built and occupied during the AD 900s. It was abandoned and deliberately filled in with refuse and soil so that the 100s room block could be built there. Excavation showed that the pithouse did not sit abandoned and fill up by slow accumulation of soil. Its disuse and filling seem to have been related events. It was filled in prior to the deposition of silts and sands by natural processes. These examples all suggest that the switch from pithouses to surface rooms was abrupt.

Surface rooms began to be built on the Mattocks site at about AD 1000 and continued until about 1130. The tree-ring dates we obtained there produced the greatest surprises. When we began work in 1974 there were no dates from any Classic Mimbres site. Each session produced additional tree-ring samples until we finally had 237 dates from the one site. Specimens recovered from other Classic Mimbres sites help confirm the pattern we found there, and much of the dating of the Classic period is based on samples from the Mattocks site. These showed that rooms were constructed throughout the 1000s and into the 1100s, with the last tree being cut down in 1117. Allowing for the likelihood that we didn't find the latest beams ever cut for the site, we believe the pueblo was abandoned by 1130, or 1150 at the very latest.

We now have a good idea of the size and layout of the settlement at this time. The Mattocks site seems to be in some ways typical of Classic Mimbres villages. It is typical in size for a major pueblo, and its layout and setting are similar to almost all comparable sites in the valley.

The Classic period Mattocks pueblo ultimately contained at least five room blocks. They ranged in size from about eight to about twenty-five rooms. Some of the blocks were linear in shape and others rather more grouped together. Some were next to the edge of the terrace and looked down on the Mimbres River floodplain 10 m below. The village seems to have centered on two large room blocks that lay approximately parallel to each other about 30 m apart. The space between these big room blocks probably served as a dance plaza. Its use as a public area seems to have had a long history, because during the preceding Pithouse period it was also empty of structures. Around these two major room blocks were smaller ones rather haphazardly arranged, often with ramadas attached to their sides. The total number of rooms on the site exceeded 100, but we believe that not all were ever occupied at one time. Therefore, we estimate that the maximum population was just under 200 people.

The typical Mimbres village may not appear to be particularly impressive. Most sites were indeed not as large or as well constructed as some of their contemporaries to the north in the Anasazi area. But on closer scrutiny the size and structure seem less important, and study reveals far more complexity in these sites than might be suspected. Indeed, we recovered evidence of important changes in social organization, the subsistence strategy, and the art of the Classic Mimbres from our work on the Mattocks site.

Modern Pueblo Indians

1   This photo, taken at the turn of
the century at one of the Hopi
pueblos, shows masked figures, or
'Kachina', dancing in a plaza. The
roofs of surrounding rooms are used
as a viewing area.

2   A dance in a plaza at Zuni
Pueblo in 1879, the terraced roofs
serving as a spectator area. Mimbres
pueblos were not multistoried, but
the roofs may have served a similar
role.

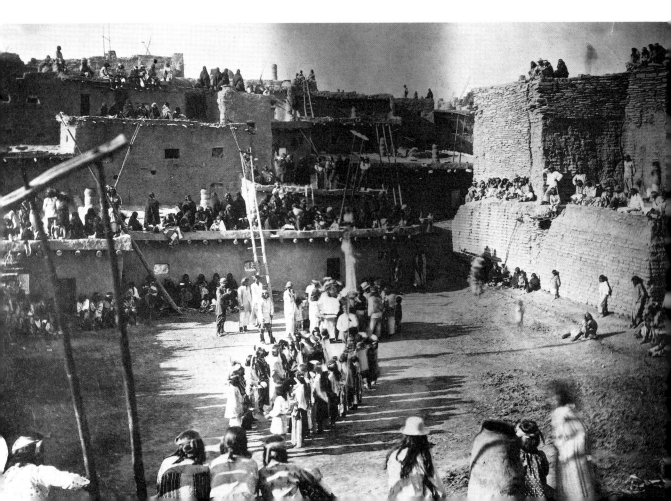

3 A view from the top of Zuni Pueblo in 1879. The roof entrance in the foreground has a hatch cover resting on end nearby. Another to the right has its cover in place. A room next to the plaza is being re-roofed. The round chimneys, topped by jars from which the bottoms have been removed, are an innovation of the historic period. Previously, smoke went out of the roof hatch.

4 Women grinding maize at Zuni Pueblo in 1899. Note the long grinding manos leaning against the wall. Elaborate bins like these are not found in the Mimbres area, but the grinding implements have changed little since ancient times.

5 An early photo of a Hopi family eating a meal of gruel or porridge from a painted bowl. The Mimbres probably used theirs similarly.

6 An 1879 photo of the courtyard at Oraibi Pueblo, a Hopi village in Arizona. The stone platform and ladder in the right foreground is the entrance to an underground ceremonial room or kiva. The stone feature to the left is probably its air shaft. Most Mimbres kivas were not totally subterranean like this one, but, we believe, extended somewhat above ground.

The plundered past. Looting Mimbres sites

7   The monetary value of Mimbres bowls has led to the wholesale looting of Mimbres village sites. Here two bulldozers destroy a fifty-room pueblo.

8   The two largest Mimbres villages were the Galaz site and the Oldtown Village site. This air-shot of Oldtown Village shows the crater-like holes left by looters. The large trenches in the upper right and the extreme left are the work of bulldozers.

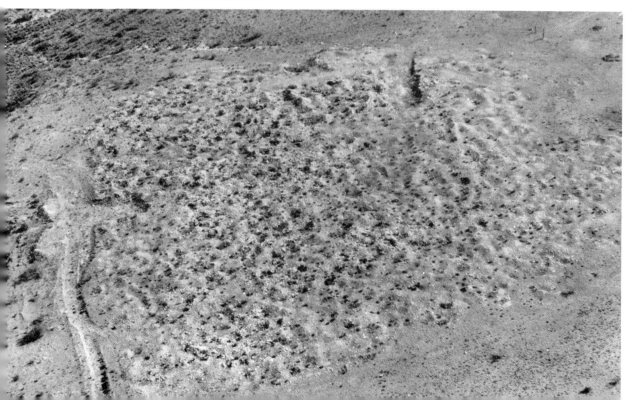

Excavations in the 1920s

9   Excavations on the Galaz site in the 1920s, conducted by the University of Minnesota.

10   The cobble walls of a kiva excavated in the 1920s by the Minnesota team. The plaster has not yet been cleaned off of the wall at the extreme right. None of these burned beams were saved for tree-ring dating.

11   A burial uncovered by the Minnesota researchers in the 1920s on the Galaz site. The bowl has just been removed from its inverted position over the body on the right. Note the impression it has left.

12 This semi-subterranean pithouse on the Mattocks site was covered over by a stone-walled surface room, and postholes and burial pits were dug into the floor. Its round hearth is shown in plate 13. Left of the hearth is a short step leading to the entrance rampway.

The recent excavations

13 This adobe-lined hearth was found in the Mattocks pithouse shown in plate 12. The shallow trough on one side may have held a pot.

14 In the transitional stage between semi-subterranean and surface architecture, the cobble walls were mostly underground, as in pithouses. Yet the architectural techniques were those of surface rooms. The plan of this structure appears in fig. 12 (page 65).

15   Pithouse 29 on the Galaz site. The ramp in the background was sealed off and replaced by another to the right, and a slab-lined hearth was built. The holes in the floor are postholes and burial pits.

16   The adobe lip at the ramp entrance to Pithouse 8 on the Galaz site would originally have extended much higher. It represents an evolved form of the bulge or lobe found on earlier structures. This Great Kiva dates to the AD 600s.

17   Pithouse 27 on the Galaz site. Visible around the edges of the excavated area are the remains of the circular pithouse replaced by the rectangular one. The remains of the old higher rampway can be seen to the right of the lower ramp, which cut through the earlier one.

18 Room 431 on the Mattocks site shows the poor
quality of the cobble walls. The floor has postholes
and burial pits. The hearth was destroyed
prehistorically.

19 Room 111 on the Mattocks site. In one corner of
the room is a rock-lined hearth, beside a large
corrugated jar. Further towards the center are two
manos.

20 Two hearths in the floor of Room 438 on the Mattocks site. The hearth on the left
was remodeled by placing stone slabs and adobe inside the original hole to make it
smaller, perhaps because wood was becoming scarce. The hearth on the right may have
been to keep pots warm.

21 The flagstone area on the edge of the 200s room block on the Mattocks site. Some was removed prehistorically and one can see how our (backfilled) test trench removed another rectangular section.

22 A small storage room on the Mattocks site. This Classic Mimbres room has poor-quality walls and an irregular floor. A single posthole can be seen in the center and a small bin in the upper left.

23 An exceptionally well-made stone hearth on the Wheaton-Smith site, whose corners were ground so as to interlock. The room was apparently a small above-ground kiva.

Arrowheads, bone tools,
and stone tools

24 Stone-tipped arrows were used for
hunting. Larger stones were knives. The
smallest arrowheads were made from
obsidian traded into the valley.

25 Bone tools were used as awls and
for weaving. Smaller pieces were
perhaps gaming pieces and beads. Very
large awl-like tools may have been
hairpins.

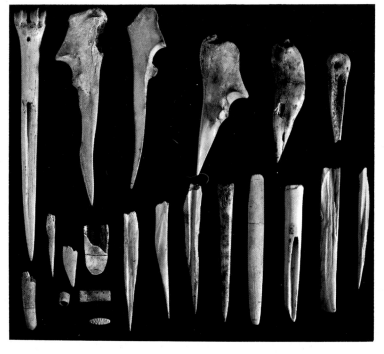

26 Stone 'hoes' are frequently found in caches of up to forty items in Classic Mimbres pueblos. We are not sure how they were used, but perhaps they served as knives to cut the fleshy leaves of the century plant.

27 Stone axes were made from a rare Pre-Cambrian rock which outcrops near the Galaz site. They would have been hafted and used to fell and trim timbers for construction.

28 Stone mauls were used to shape stones into metates, for example. Many mauls were simply re-used axe heads, but this specimen was especially made from vesicular basalt.

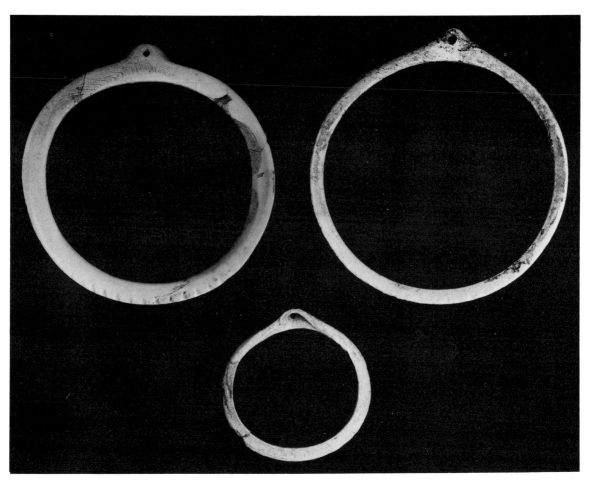

29   Shell bracelets made from marine clam shells. These were imported in finished form from the Hohokam area of Arizona.

30   Copper bells from various Mimbres sites. They were imported from Mexico and must have been very valuable items.

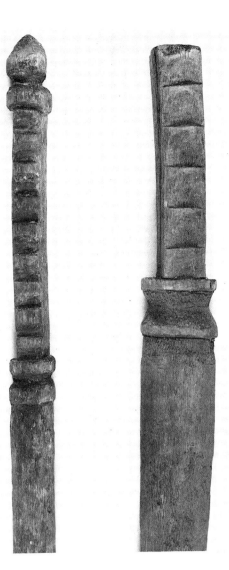

31   A sherd from a Mimbres bowl ground into the
shape of a fish, and a fragment of incised stone
pendant.

32   Wooden staffs from caves in New Mexico. These
pieces, with round heads and notched 'hilts', have been
found over much of the Southwest. They are probably
the 'swords' or 'wands' depicted in various painted
bowls, such as in plates 71, 78, and XIII.

Ornaments and luxury items

33   A palette in the shape of a bear's
paw from the excavations at the
Galaz site.

34   Over half the vessels made by the Mimbres were unpainted utility jars. This one is corrugated. The remains of soot in the indentations show that it was used to cook over a fire.

35   A very unusual pitcher from the Late Pithouse period. Plastic elements or incisions were occasionally used as decorative devices.

36   A canteen-shaped jar from the post-Mimbres period, when very few pieces were painted. The design is much less refined than on Mimbres bowls.

37 A small pitcher from the Late Pithouse period, *c.* AD 900. The simple corrugations on the neck are typical. Probably used for serving and consuming gruel-like foods.

38 A large jar with incised and cord-marked designs from the post-Mimbres period. Incisions largely replaced the painted designs of the preceding Classic Mimbres period.

39 A large Classic Mimbres painted jar. Although about 10 per cent of all painted vessels were jars, very few complete specimens have survived.

40 Besides large jars, the Mimbres made smaller ones which have been called seed jars. They were rarely used as funerary offerings, so few have survived.

9 The Classic Mimbres village

We can now broadly reconstruct the nature of Classic period villages in the Mimbres Valley and adjacent regions. Between AD 1000 and 1130 there existed about a dozen large villages in the valley proper. The Mattocks, Galaz, and *fig. 20* Swarts ruins are good examples. They had from 2 to 8 room blocks each, and contained from 50 to perhaps 200 rooms. The population of any one village probably never exceeded 300 people. These settlements were spaced about 3 miles apart along the river. Between them were many smaller sites, some of which were small villages with only a single room block and containing less than 25 rooms. Most of the small sites, however, were probably only seasonally used and were neither constructed nor used like the village sites.[25]

20 An artist's reconstruction of the Galaz pueblo during the Classic Mimbres period, at about AD 1100. The area between the room blocks may have served as a plaza where ceremonies were held.

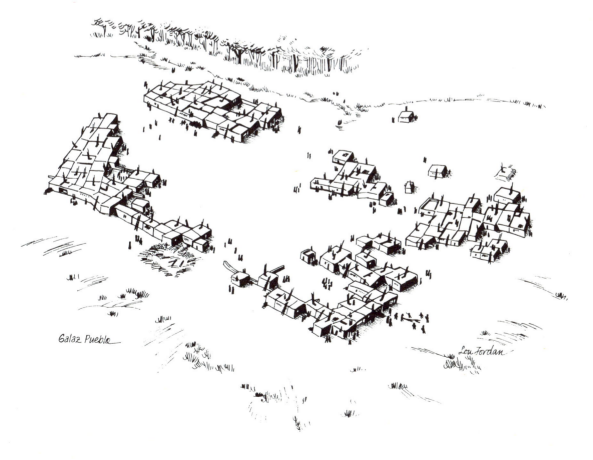

Galaz Pueblo

Lou Jordan

Their buildings were constructed with only a few courses of masonry; the rest of the walls would have been of poles and mud. They lack hearths, burials, and artifact types which are found in the permanent villages. They seem to be summer field houses and were built as places to watch the fields and to store crops temporarily at harvest time.

In the desert area, where the Mimbres River flows out on to the open plains, less than half a dozen major villages stood where high water tables or springs made farming possible. Again, small sites were found between them. These probably were used as stations where wild resources such as mesquite beans were collected. The mountains around the valley contained additional sites. For the most part these were associated with small areas where farming was possible. Small dams were occasionally used to improve water flow and soil conditions. Some of the few relatively flat and fertile areas in the mountains were occupied by a larger village. Such settlements rarely attained fifty rooms in size, and usually had twenty-five or less. To the west of the Mimbres Valley several large villages existed along the major water courses. Here the pattern found in the Mimbres Valley was repeated, only at a smaller scale. These areas each contained three or four large villages with smaller and usually seasonal sites interspersed among them.

Our work on the Mattocks site and other Classic Mimbres pueblos, and our re-evaluation of the field notes from earlier excavations, led us to understand to some degree the composition, growth and social organization of the Mimbres villages.

Our reconstructions are heavily based on architectural information. Archaeologists study prehistoric architecture for a variety of reasons. One reason, of course, is that structural remains are frequently well preserved and capable of yielding large quantities of information. Some aspects of architecture are purely functional, but others, such as the layout or the shape of hearths, may reflect differences in cultural affiliation. Beyond this, structures can tell us quite a bit about the adaptive strategy of their inhabitants. The permanence of buildings and the area set aside for storage give us insight into the subsistence strategy itself. At a still different level, architecture can reveal information on the social organization of the community. Are all structures the same size, or are a few larger and more elaborate than the rest? Are there areas where specific tasks were performed, such as pottery-making workshops? How large was the group that built and used each structure or group of buildings?

Until recently these kinds of questions had not been considered for the Classic Mimbres pueblos. The reasons were complex. Several important sites had been excavated, but most of the useful information remained hidden away in unpublished notes and maps. Also, previous researchers did not seem to care how the Mimbres organized their lives, so many questions were just not asked. As a result of providing new information and of finding and analyzing the old unpublished material, some rather interesting patterns have emerged.

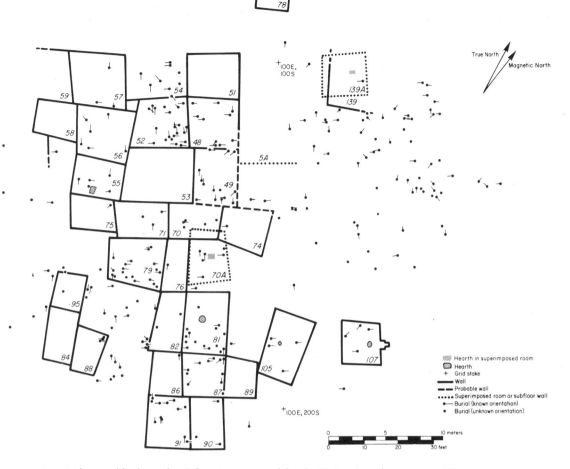

21 *A typical room block on the Galaz site excavated by the University of Minnesota. The irregularly shaped rooms and haphazard layout are apparent. The isolated structure off the southeast corner of the room block was a small kiva. Burials were found in the room block area, concentrated to the east.*

As we have seen, the Classic Mimbres period witnessed a shift from semi-subterranean pithouses to above-ground, multiroomed pueblos. The Galaz site shows that technologically the change was a small one; the methods used in building surface rooms existed by the latter part of the Late Pithouse period. Did the switch to surface rooms reflect a new social organization, with large groups of people rapidly coming together? Or was it no more than an architectural shift, with little social change accompanying it? In particular, did everybody abandon their pithouses and quickly build large multiroomed *fig. 21* pueblos, or did these pueblos grow at a slow pace? Why were there such differences in size between the smallest and the largest of the excavated room blocks – from a minimum of eight rooms to over fifty?

Even though most of these questions had not yet been asked, archaeologists turned to the Swarts ruin as a model for a typical Mimbres pueblo, principally because the report on the excavations there produced the only published map of completely excavated room blocks. The site was simply assumed to be typical. The Swarts ruin had 2 very large room blocks of 45 and 70 rooms. These are the largest roughly rectangular blocks found at any Classic Mimbres pueblo, including Mattocks, Galaz, and other sites studied by the Mimbres Project. In fact, much smaller room blocks are found at these and other sites, and they were often rather linear in shape.

We have recently resolved the apparent inconsistency between the Swarts and other Mimbres villages, and in the process have learned a great deal about their growth. A restudy of the information from the field notes on the Swarts ruin showed that its history was similar to that of other sites. It was only the final appearance of the room blocks that was unusual. The Swarts pueblo *fig. 22* actually began as 6 small rooms, or clusters of them, typically including 3 to 5 rooms. There were about 17 rooms on the site as a whole. New rooms were rapidly added to the initial blocks. These additions soon resulted in blocks of up to 14 rooms. There were still 6 separate blocks when the settlement contained 32 rooms. Its make-up at this time is very similar to other sites. Subsequent developments led to its unusual size and internal structure. Further additions caused the room blocks to grow together, until only two separate blocks remained by the last building phase.

We now suspect that it was the unique setting of the Swarts village that led to this situation. It is the only Classic Mimbres pueblo known that was built on the floodplain itself. Why this vulnerable spot was chosen we do not know, but we can be sure that the valuable farm land surrounding it would not have been readily wasted. Other Mimbres villages, on the terrace above the river, expanded extensively over ground which was not valuable farmland. The Swarts community instead added rooms in the spaces between the room blocks, which did not increase the extent of the village and therefore did not destroy any usable farm areas. The result was that the room blocks grew together until they coalesced into two massive room blocks. This configuration was reached long before the pueblo reached its maximal extent. As further growth took place, no new room blocks were begun; the pueblo continued to grow by adding rooms onto the two existing blocks.

This reconstruction of the development of the Swarts pueblo is supported by similar growth patterns at other sites. There, room blocks also began small and grew by accretion. The first phase of the Swarts pueblo had only some seventeen rooms. This seems to have been too few to have housed all the people who must have lived in the pithouse village underlying the surface pueblo. It may be that not all the people abandoned their pithouses and built surface rooms at the same time.

If we look at the Swarts pueblo before the room blocks began to coalesce *figs 23–4* (*fig. 22*) we can ask what type of family groups might have been living in each of these six room blocks. Typically, these had eight rooms and housed perhaps sixteen people. This is about the size of a large extended family, which might

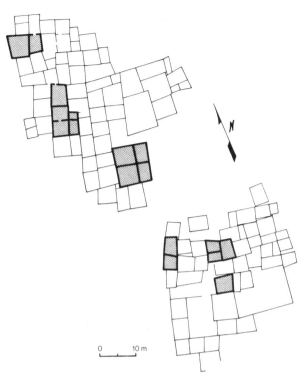

22 (Right) The Swarts ruin is the only Mimbres village that has been completely excavated. The pueblo probably grew from AD 1000 to 1130. The first construction phase consisted of six small clusters of rooms. The location of the final configuration is also shown.

23 (Below left) Later in the history of the Swarts village, further rooms were added to the original clusters, but six discrete room blocks still existed. The final configuration of the village is also shown.

24 (Below right) Late in the history of the Swarts village, the room blocks grew into two large room blocks; still later, additional rooms were constructed completing the final configuration.

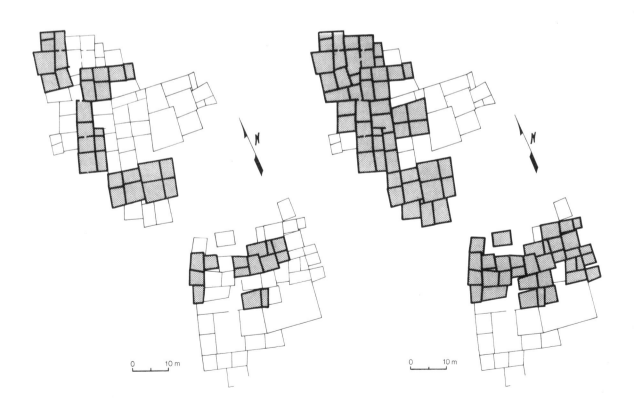

have had an elderly parent or two, and their grown and married children as well as the children of this second generation.

Today in the Southwest the Pueblo Indians are matrilocal; the daughters remain in their mothers' households and the sons move into the homes of their new wives. While we have no evidence that the Mimbres were matrilocal, it is quite likely they were unilocal, so that either sons or daughters moved into new households when they married. Under these circumstances we should not expect all households or extended families to be of the same size. A couple that had only sons would see them marry and move away. The remaining household would be composed of the couple, perhaps living in only a few rooms. In the south of the Swarts village were two room blocks, one with two rooms and the other with four, which may reflect this very situation. Conversely, the successful raising of three daughters might have resulted in quite a large household. Such a residence group might have included two grandparents, their daughters, their three husbands and a number of children. The large room blocks in the north of the Swarts site may have housed such families.

Everything we know so far supports the supposition that Mimbres room blocks were occupied by small groups, of the varied sizes we would expect from unilocal residence groups. In some villages the blocks may have grown together, but it is unlikely that the resulting larger units represent a different form of corporate organization. The extended family, or unilocal lineage spanning three generations, probably remained the basic economic unit of Mimbres society throughout the Classic period.

The change from pithouse to surface rooms does not seem to be the result of a major sociological change, but it may indicate a significant new adaptation. During the Late Pithouse period, new generations probably set up their own households in separate new pithouses, while in the Classic Mimbres period, households may have spanned several generations. Such pooling of labor and food would have resulted in greater productive efficiency, and it is possible that a potential for more craft specialization arose from this new residence pattern.

What evidence do we have for social organization above that of the minimal kin-group which probably occupied a room block? We have seen that in the Late Pithouse period, large communal structures are found at the larger sites. It was argued earlier that the ritual activities conducted in these great kivas served to integrate the villages. While some of these structures were probably still employed at the beginning of the Classic Mimbres period, they soon fell into disuse and were abandoned. There were therefore no architectural structures that could have housed even a fraction of the population of one of the Classic Mimbres villages. Nevertheless, it is very unlikely that these integrating institutions disappeared completely.

We now believe that merely the location of this ritual activity changed. The public ceremonials seem to have gone above ground and out into the open.

Other Mogollon sites, a little later in time, show clear evidence that the large central plazas were a place for public religious activities. We may well expect a similar arrangement to have existed in the Classic Mimbres villages. One obvious reason for such a change is that, as the population expanded, it would have been increasingly difficult to build a structure large enough to house all the people who would have wanted to view a ceremony. Holding assemblies outside would have eliminated this problem.

Today, among the Puebloan Indians of the Southwest, public ceremonial dances are held out of doors in plazas surrounded by multi-storied room blocks. Frequently, the rooftops of the room blocks are used by spectators. Mimbres room blocks may have served a similar function.

Most major Mimbres pueblos have a central open area or plaza bordered by two or more room blocks. Their size is about what we find in the historic and modern pueblos. Sites like the Mattocks and the Swarts are good examples of villages with plazas which are not bordered on all sides. If we look at the Swarts pueblo during its early stages (*fig. 23*), however, we see that two of the northern room blocks form a U shape. Could this have been a deliberate building plan to define a space for public ceremonies? At the Galaz site there were three room blocks that formed a well-defined plaza area, as can be seen in our reconstruction (*fig. 20*). Apart from the flagstone enclosure at the Mattocks site, we have found no features in the open areas themselves that help to confirm this interpretation, but the arrival of the plaza remains a highly plausible explanation for the disappearance of great kivas.

The transition to plazas was only one of several changes in ceremonial architecture at this time. For the first time, in the Classic period, we have evidence of an entirely new form of ceremonial room. Previously, the kivas had been large enough to accomodate most of the people in a village. With the advent of surface rooms we find small kivas which could have held only ten or twelve people at the most. Such buildings are well known from this time in the Anasazi area.

Our recent discovery and understanding of these small structures in the Mimbres area is a good example of how archaeological knowledge progresses. They were first reported for the Mimbres area in 1927 by the Cosgroves, and other examples were excavated in the late 1920s and 1930s.[26] Although semi-subterranean, they did not look like ordinary pithouses. They did not have ramp entrances, but were entered from an opening in the roof. The only other opening was a vertical shaft which permitted air circulation. These are features normally associated with kivas elsewhere in the Southwest.

fig. 25

These structures excavated by the Cosgroves were ignored by archaeologists, and with some reason. No one had a really good idea of their age. Were they perhaps aberrant domestic pithouses built during the Late Pithouse period? Or were they used during the Classic period and thus contemporary with surface pueblos? If the latter were true these semi-subterranean structures would more likely be special-function rooms. In the Anasazi area,

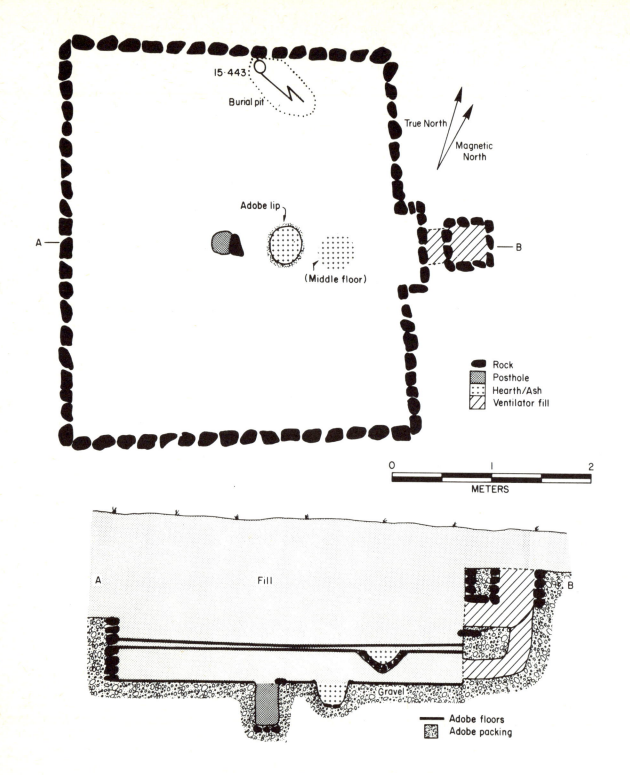

15·443

Burial pit

True North

Magnetic North

Adobe lip

(Middle floor)

A

B

Rock
Posthole
Hearth/Ash
Ventilator fill

0   1   2
METERS

A   Fill   B

Gravel

—— Adobe floors
⠿ Adobe packing

25 *The plan and profile of a kiva from the Galaz site, excavated by the University of Minnesota. Although semi-subterranean, it had stone walls. An air shaft brought fresh air to the hearth. After the original room was constructed, a new floor was laid about 40 cm above the original one and a new hearth built. This required filling up the bottom of the original air shaft and cutting a new entrance into the room. This second floor was subsequently covered by another new floor, but no hearth was found on the upper floor.*

semi-subterranean kivas had a series of specialized features, including large recesses and roof-support pillars adjacent to the outer walls. No such features were found in the Mimbres examples. Moreover, there seemed to be no other evidence that supported the idea that these structures had a special function.

As so often in archaeology, all the evidence needed to prove the existence of these kivas had long been available. But it had not been seen because it had not been looked for. The Mimbres Project's excavation of Pithouse 410 on the Mattocks site in 1977 finally changed the situation. One of our long exploratory trenches revealed a pithouse near the 400s room block. The initial stages of the excavation of this structure yielded nothing surprising; a rectangular pithouse typical of the Late Pithouse period was uncovered.

Soon, however, it became clear that the pithouse was not typical of those dating from the AD 800s or 900s. The original rampway had been closed up prehistorically and replaced by an airshaft. Other evidence of remodeling was also found – hardly surprisingly, since the original entrance had been sealed and a means of entering from the roof must have been required. When we examined the pottery from the building we found Late Pithouse period types, but also considerable pottery from the Classic period. Final confirmation of the date of the structure came from tree-ring samples. These confirmed that the structure had been remodeled or at least occupied in the AD 1000s – the Classic period.

We now had solid evidence for a structure that had been built as a pithouse, but remodeled into something like a kiva during the Classic period. Almost at the same time, another similar building turned up at a small site at the very upper end of the valley. In this case, it was clear the structure had been built during the Classic period. It was a very deep pithouse, designed from its inception to have an air vent and a roof entrance.

We now became convinced that these small kivas were used during the Classic Mimbres period. We reasoned that if we had found two of them, many more must have been excavated by the earlier projects. Roger Anyon, who had been studying the Late Pithouse great kivas, began to review the original field notes of excavations at various sites and quickly discovered that these small kivas were quite common.[27] He found examples not only of pithouses having been remodeled into kivas, but also of structures of this kind originally built as kivas. These other examples had gone unrecognized because they were almost all unpublished and not known to other archaeologists.

Roger Anyon then discovered a fact that provided additional support for the interpretation of these structures as kivas. He found they were associated with room blocks, and often situated near or exactly on the edge of one of the rooms. No room block ever had more than one of these structures in use at any one time. Whenever the information we possessed about a particular room block was fairly complete, we almost always found an associated kiva. This was the critical pattern; a proper Classic Mimbres room block had from about eight to twenty rooms and a kiva. Not only were the kivas similar to those in the Anasazi area, but the pattern of one for each room block also prevailed at that time in the northern area.

The few room blocks that lacked an associated semi-subterranean kiva had a special-purpose surface room which seems to have taken its place. These rooms were located on the peripheries of room blocks and were usually quite large. They also had atypical roof-support systems, but their hearths were perhaps the most distinctive feature. These were large and elaborate affairs, reminiscent of the hearths found in the great kivas of the preceding period.

Our excavations revealed such a structure and hearth at the Wheaton-Smith site. This medium-size Mimbres pueblo lay on a tributary to the Mimbres River, and never attained the size of the pueblos located along the main drainage. This site had only one room block. In one corner was a very large plate 23   room we interpreted as a ceremonial room. Its extra-large hearth consisted of four stone slabs. The ends of each slab had been cut and ground so that they interlocked at the corners of the hearth.

These smaller ceremonial structures obviously represent a considerable departure from the larger great kivas of the Late Pithouse period and the plazas of the Classic Mimbres pueblos. The small kivas were possibly used by each kin group (or part of each kin group) which occupied the room block with which it was associated.

Among the modern Puebloan communities of the Southwest, kivas are used by different societies whose limits cut across kin groups. The men who are members of a particular society use that society's kiva as a retreat; certain private ceremonies are also conducted there. Each society contains members who belong to different kin groups (lineages and clans) and therefore to different households. Thus, the kivas are not associated with a particular household or room block.[28]

The association of each room block with a small semi-subterranean kiva, and later in the Classic period the presence of a small kiva within each room block, suggests that these kivas were used by the ceremonial participants of that kin group. This would account for their small size, and for their consistent presence in or near each room block.

It does seem clear that the Classic Mimbres period witnessed a change in the structure of the community. During the Late Pithouse period we have evidence only for household organizational units and for single-village systems. The Classic period still had households, but these seem to have incorporated a group which required a large architectural unit – the room block. It was suggested above that plazas replaced great kivas as the locus of ceremonial activities of the village as a whole. Thus, some form of social institution which integrates the village still seems to have operated during the Classic period, although the evidence for it is less conclusive.

We see then that Mimbres villages are fairly complex. Two kinds of domestic rooms existed: living rooms and storage rooms. Roofed outdoor work areas, or ramadas, were also common. Ceremonialism probably had several components, a public or pan-village aspect and a more restricted or private aspect. Besides the need to define plaza spaces by building room blocks around them, there was no overall planning effort in the villages; growth was haphazard and unregulated. What we don't find in these villages is also important. We find no evidence for differences in the size or elaborateness of domestic rooms; no specialized work areas that would suggest the presence of an elite group of full-time craftsmen; and no evidence for a priestly caste or for the concentration of religious offices within one kin group. The distribution of ceremonial structures within the community indicates that ritual activities were important for all segments of the community. Each of the groups living in the various room blocks within the settlements played some role. In the light of this reconstructed picture, Classic Mimbres villages have much in common with simple horticultural societies elsewhere in prehistory. But other features mark this society as being unique of its kind. This will be the subject of the following chapter.

10 Mimbres painted pottery

The painted bowls of the Classic period are the most distinctive and remarkable class of artifact produced by the Mimbres.[29] One of the mysteries about this society has been and continues to be why they produced such extraordinary pottery. The development of the Mimbres Archive has helped unravel the pottery style, but we still feel that the full potential for understanding Mimbres bowl painting has barely been realized.

We have already discussed the slow evolution of early pottery, until the development of the ceramic type called Boldface Black on White. During the first 350 years (from AD 200 to 550) only plain undecorated wares were produced. The next 100 years saw the addition of polished red bowls and jars. Around AD 650 painted pottery was first produced. Evolution was still slow; the first bowls were painted with red designs on brown backgrounds –
plates VII, X
Mogollon Red on Brown – which continued to be made with little change for 75 to 100 years. In about AD 750 the tempo of change began to pick up. The red on brown pottery evolved into a red on white pottery – Three Circle Red on White. Within 25 to 50 years this in turn developed into a black on white ceramic tradition. Once this color scheme was established it remained constant for almost 350 years. It was now the designs themselves that began to change rapidly.

The above sequence of the basic features of Mimbres pottery was formulated by Emil Haury in the 1930s. The black on white pottery which began to be produced around AD 800 had traditionally been divided into two ceramic types on the basis of design characteristics. The earlier pottery was Boldface Black on White, characterized by more 'primitive' or less well-executed designs. Certain motifs were typically found on Boldface bowls, the designs often covering the entire bowl, right up to its rim. This type was correctly recognized as having been replaced by Classic Mimbres Black on White, which has finely executed painting, the designs of which are separated from the bowl rim by a single band, or several concentric ones, just below the rim.

We can now see that this traditional typology is too crude to tell us much about the development of the ceramic tradition or the communities that produced it. Pottery design evolved in a very regular and subtle fashion with essentially no abrupt changes. The earliest Boldface Black on White was simple and bold in its layout. Interlocking scrolls were common, and a wavy or

squiggly line was used to make spirals and concentric circles. These designs, plate 42
which were organized in a single field covering the entire bowl, were followed
by a quadrant layout which continued in use for over one hundred years. An plate 46
important development at about this time was the use of squiggly lines as filler
or hachures in fields bordered by straight lines.

These changes occurred before A D 900. At about that date the predominant
designs were so distinct from earlier Boldface wares that a different name was
used, the Oak Grove style. The title was proposed by a local amateur, while we
originally called this design the transitional style. But we decided that the
nomenclature was becoming unwieldy, and proposed calling the Boldface
style 'Phase I' and the Oak Grove or transitional style simply 'Phase II'.
Because the evolution was gradual, many bowls which are intermediate in
style do exist. The hallmark of Phase II was the use of straight lines as hachure
elements, which are much narrower than the lines which form the border of
the field.

During the period at which the Phase II style predominated, some features
of Hohokam ceramic tradition were adopted by the Mimbres. An elongated
bowl, a common Hohokam shape, began to be produced in the Mimbres.
These 'gravy-boat'-shaped vessels also tended to have motifs similar to those plate 41
found on Hohokam pottery. This vessel shape, however, was never popular
and quickly disappeared.

Another Hohokam influence was more interesting. The Mimbres almost
invariably organized the painted designs to reflect the shape of the bowl itself.
This is especially noticeable in the later Classic style where concentric circles
or whole designs would be painted around the rim. But even in the early
Boldface pottery, the painted designs would be organized in a circular layout.
The Hohokam, on the other hand, frequently painted their bowls so that the
design flowed outwards from the center without adjusting to the circular form
of the vessel. This trait was briefly picked up by Mimbres painters in the late
800s and early 900s. Bowls were painted as if the design had been made on a
large flat surface, of which a portion had then been cut out and laid onto the
interior surface of the pot. The patterns were usually repetitive, in one or more
directions away from the center, and were conceptually similar to modern
wallpaper, hence our use of the term wallpaper design.

Such atypical layouts are possibly the idiosyncratic work of only a few
individuals. What is important is that a foreign shape and design were not
successfully incorporated into the Mimbres repertoire. Thus, although there
was contact between the Mimbres potters and those of surrounding regions,
few features were adopted for any length of time.

After A D 900, the rate of change in Mimbres design began to increase. Two
notable new developments soon occurred. For the first time a circular field in
the center of the bowl was left unpainted. A second development was that the plate 50
painted design no longer extended to the rim of the bowl. It was bordered by a
line just below the rim. Somewhat later this thick line or band was separated plates 51–2

plates IV, 53 from the principal painted design and became free standing. Concurrent with this separation of design from rim, the hachure evolved so that its own lines and those enclosing them were of the same narrow width.

Hachure with a fine border and rim bands are hallmarks of the Classic Mimbres, or Phase III style. It developed around AD 1000. Mimbres design now changes rapidly, developing in a number of different directions, employing new motifs and combining them in new ways, so that this part of the ceramic sequence can be likened to an artistic explosion. The rapidity and complexity of these developments have made the dating of the sequence much more difficult.

plate 54 The Phase III style at first used only one rim band to separate the field of painted design from the bowl rim, but very quickly a great variety of thick and thin band combinations were employed. But for certain motifs we have been able to see more fine gradation in the evolution of the style. A good example is the herringbone-like motif shown in plate 51, which evolved from one in the Phase II style.

Figurative or representational painting followed a parallel evolution. It began simply in the Boldface or Phase I style and increased in complexity and diversity through the later phases. Only a few figurative bowls were painted in Boldface. Phase II saw a marked increase in the use of figurative painting, with the horned toad or lizard and the bird as fairly common motifs. At the beginning of the Classic period, the representational style also proliferates into a burst of variety. A plethora of animals, people, and group scenes appear.

plates VI, XI, 58–60, 63–4, 66 Fully one-third of the mortuary vessels of this period have figurative motifs.

Although the style developed increasingly rapidly, we have enough chronological control over this evolution to consider it in terms of the lives of the potters themselves. Phase II lasted no more than one hundred years and the change to the Classic style or Phase III occurred within a generation. Thus, someone learning to paint pottery at the age of fifteen and continuing to paint until the age of forty-five or fifty would have lived through considerable modifications in the painted-pottery tradition. Some bowls may have been kept for many years and have been eventually treated as heirlooms, so potters must have been able to see or remember a considerable temporal span of pottery making. They must have been fully aware of changing design styles.

We often think of such an art evolving very slowly, with most painters copying known and accepted canons, and change coming about inadvertently. This did not happen in the Mimbres area. The evolution of design during the latter part of the Mimbres occupation was so rapid compared to the life-span of the individual, that we must acknowledge that innovation resulted from a conscious effort. When we couple this with the fact that no two Mimbres bowls are alike, it seems probable that change and variety were important for their own sake. Whatever the reason, Mimbres designs were more varied and evolved more rapidly than those of other contemporary Southwestern peoples.

Mimbres figurative painting

Mimbres figurative painting is such an unusual and rich tradition that it has already received considerable attention. It is frequently asked what the designs plate IX mean or represent. This is not a frivolous question. Were some of the images symbols of the potter's kin group? Such totemic signs indicating clan membership appear in various media among other North American cultural groups, for example the famous totem or house poles of the Northwestern coastal groups. Do the bowls show scenes from everyday life, or were they important religious or mythological depictions?

Trying to determine what was in the mind of the makers of artifacts is perhaps the hardest of all archaeological problems, but we do have a few threads of information which shed some light on the question. All solutions must be viewed with extreme caution as it is easy for us to interpret these paintings through our own cultural background.

We have approached the problem of how the bowls functioned in society from two directions. One approach has been to study how they were distributed over the Mimbres area. Which types of bowls were found at different sites? Which individuals were they buried with? We expected the choice of bowl to be dictated in part by the deceased's place in society. Thus we expected women to be treated differently from men, and so on. Also, each room block, or even each village in some cases, may have been occupied by a different clan, each of which may have had their own totemic symbols depicted on the bowls.

Our work in identifying patterns of this kind has had only limited results. Some motifs, such as deer or lizards, are relatively more common in certain sites than in others, but no motif is exclusively used in any particular village. Moreover, we do not see concentrations of motifs in limited parts of villages, or even within particular rooms. We do find, surprisingly, that children were buried with a disproportionate number of figurative bowls when compared with adults, but again we can find little evidence that particular motifs were associated with either males or females or with particular age groups.

Our second approach has been to try to understand better the motifs themselves. This approach has been quite successful. Our major effort has involved the interpretation of figurative scenes by Hopi Indians of northern Arizona.[30] This study was conducted by Lois Weslowski, based on interviews with Hopi consultants. While there is little need to suspect a direct relationship between the prehistoric Mimbres and the historic Hopi, the Hopi certainly share a broad common history and similar adaptation to the Southwestern environment.

The Hopi consultants were extremely astute observers and taught us to look more carefully at the motifs, and to view them without reference to Western artistic canons. Several Hopi felt that some of the abstract designs on the bowls were probably actual objects used by the Mimbres and were not imaginary.

This opinion encouraged us to examine these motifs again, and led us to some interesting conclusions.

plates XIII, 32, 71, 78 There are at least twelve known Mimbres bowls which depict what we have labeled the 'sword' motif. All are depicted according to standard conventions. They have a 'handle' with a round 'pommel', and a wide 'hilt'. The 'blade' is almost always shown with a herringbone pattern while the tip is plain. It is intriguing that some of the 'swords' are shown half as tall as a man; others are shown little larger than an insect.

Dr J. J. Brody of the Maxwell Museum of Anthropology at the University of New Mexico has recently remarked that archaeologically recovered wooden artifacts both from the Mimbres area and from Chaco Canyon in northwest New Mexico are extremely similar to the Mimbres painted 'swords'.[31] These artifacts, almost a meter long, appear to be nonutilitarian, probably ceremonial objects. They may well be stylized versions of everyday wooden digging sticks used for farming. Thus, the Mimbres depicted real objects, but not always showing their actual size. Modification of scale is seen in other motifs as well.

Another bowl scene also shows that paintings may be less imaginary than first appears. A number of bowls show men with very large fish. Some show men seemingly being eaten by them, while others show a man spearing or carrying one. The spearing scenes were originally baffling because of the size of the fish. These seemed to be either mythological scenes or proof that the Mimbres were aware of the large fish of the oceans. Upon investigation, however, it turned out that a species known as the squaw fish, about 1.3 m long, was plentiful along the lower Gila River in the 1800s: not in the Mimbres area, but quite nearby. So it becomes much easier to understand how a potter with some imagination could stretch one to the size of the Mimbreño catching it. Even the Classic Mimbres, it seems, had their fish stories.

plates 65, 79 The representational paintings were not all of realistic scenes. Clearly some are imaginary. Mammals with fish-tails, bird-wings, and human-like heads are shown, as well as other impossible scenes. But to say that some bowl scenes are non-realistic is not very informative. We are beginning to realize that it is dangerous to assume too quickly that an image we do not understand is mythological. There are often rational explanations.

The Hopi provided us with even more important insight into Mimbres art. They consistently saw evidence in representational scenes for the relationship between different groups within the society and between man and nature. They interpreted scenes which included more than one animal as showing relationships between clans of which the animals were the totemic symbols. Where one animal was eating or perhaps hunting another, the Hopi would see the relationship between the two clans. Or they would see that the animals plate 67 were discussing their role in helping mankind. The Hopi interpreted many scenes as showing how the lives of man and animal were intertwined; the symbiotic rather than the adversarial aspect of the relationship was stressed.

Painted bowls

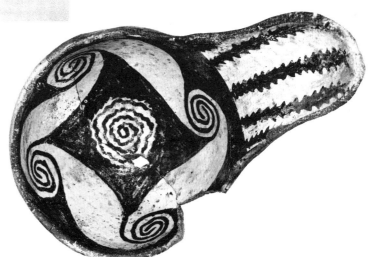

41 An unusual and early rectangular bowl made in the 900s.

42 An early Boldface bowl with scrolls and concentric wavy lines. Early bowls were rarely 'killed' by piercing a hole in the bottom.

43 A rare ladle in the Boldface style.

44 The scrolls of the early Boldface style evolved into elegant designs which can be viewed either as positive or negative imagery. The hole in the bottom of the bowl, commonly referred to as a 'kill' hole, was made when the vessel was included in a burial.

45 An early 900s bowl in which the geometric scrolls flow into feet.

46 A late Boldface bowl with a quadrant layout. The typical filler elements are now wavy lines.

47 A bowl made in the 900s. The design is typically divided into four repetitive quadrants.

48, 49 Two bowls dating to the 900s, with fine hachured geometric designs bounded by wide or fat lines.

50 A bowl from the transition period before the Classic Mimbres.

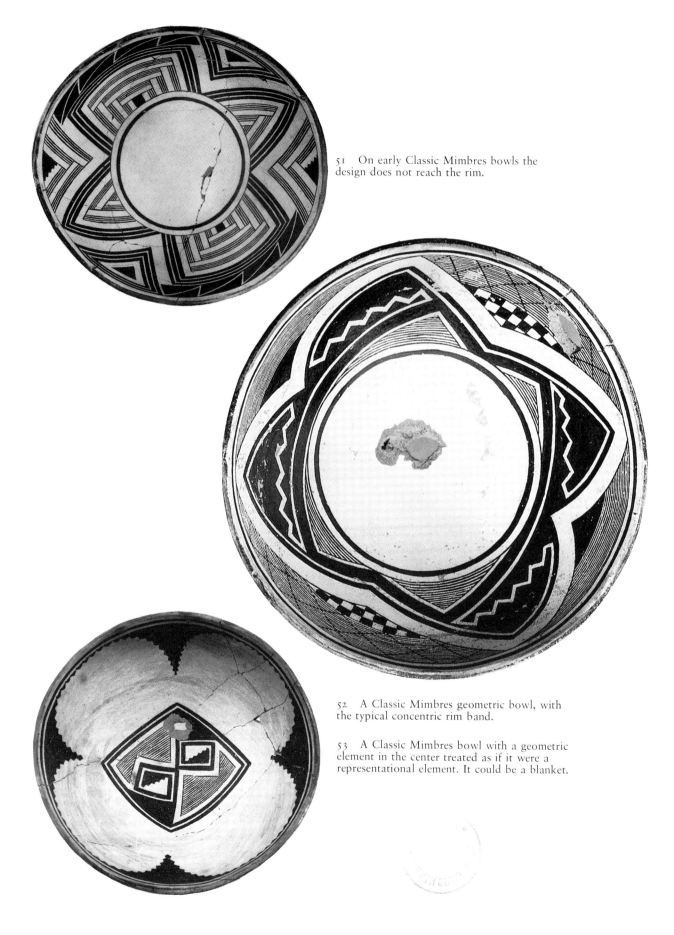

51 On early Classic Mimbres bowls the design does not reach the rim.

52 A Classic Mimbres geometric bowl, with the typical concentric rim band.

53 A Classic Mimbres bowl with a geometric element in the center treated as if it were a representational element. It could be a blanket.

54   A Classic Mimbres geometric bowl.

55 An early and uncommon representational bowl, probably of the 900s. Fish, frequently portrayed later, were rarely eaten.

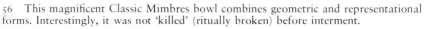

56 This magnificent Classic Mimbres bowl combines geometric and representational forms. Interestingly, it was not 'killed' (ritually broken) before interment.

57 An early naturalistic bowl, showing a front-facing bird and a lizard – common representations during the formative period of this style.

58 A Classic Mimbres bowl from the Mattocks site.

59 The Mimbres frequently combined geometric and representational figures. Here an insect appears in the center of a geometric design.

60   Two ducks are shown here, apparently in flight, attached by three wavy lines.

61   A bird executed in a negative style. As always, the design is in black paint
on a white background.

62 A Classic Mimbres representational bowl.

63 This Classic Mimbres bowl, from the 400s room block on the Mattocks site, depicts two siamese rabbits. The multiple kill holes are very uncommon.

64 A Classic Mimbres bowl with a ring-tailed cat.

65 A mythological figure, half rabbit and half rattlesnake.

66 A Classic Mimbres bowl with a frog. It has three kill holes.

67   A dog and turkey shown in perspective. The turkey's feet are hidden by the dog, so the turkey is in the background. Hopi consultants suggest they are having a conversation, judging by the turned head of the dog. They may represent different clans, with the imagery symbolizing their relationship.

68   This Classic Mimbres bowl subtly integrates representational and geometric elements. The two bighorn sheep are stepping into the geometric patterns.

69 A Classic Mimbres bowl from the Mattocks ruin.

70 Is the dog sitting on the head of this elegantly drawn grasshopper, or is it in the background? The unusual size relationships of the figures may signify an aspect of mythology or legend.

71 A rabbit with a sword or wand. The wand is depicted in various sizes and represents a real wooden ceremonial artifact made by the Mimbres (see plate 32).

72 One of a handful of image-reversal designs. This can be seen as four bird-like or ghost-like figures, or four humans with a common head.

73　This very intriguing Mimbres bowl shows
two animals apparently linked to an egg by
umbilical cords. The figure inside the egg may be
a human with a humped back. The Hopi felt that
the box patterns on either side of the egg were
symbols of maize. A face is also formed, with the
human figure's eye and the negative circle as its
eyes. The legs are the nose and mouth.

74　Perhaps one of the most intriguing of all
Mimbres bowls, for the long-necked crane reverses
into a human head. This motif appears on other
bowls, such as in plate V.

75　An anthropomorphic figure in
'negative' painting, with black areas
painted onto a white background.

76 This elegant combination of a snake and a man demonstrates the Mimbres use of perspective. The hollow body of the man shows that the snake is in front, since it overlaps this part of the man's body.

77 This decapitation scene may reflect Mesoamerican influences. The person performing the ritual is holding what is probably a knife and is wearing a horned-serpent costume – maybe the local equivalent of Quetzalcoatl, a feathered horned serpent of the Mesoamerican pantheon.

78 One of a series of wand or sword motifs (see also plate 71). Here it is anthropomorphized. The arms hold various objects and a feather is worn. The other figure is female, as shown by the sash. She carries a basket and wears a headband and bracelets. She also appears to wear face paint or tatoos. This probably depicts a particular legend or story in the Mimbres oral history.

79 A fish-like man on a Classic Mimbres bowl from the Wheaton-Smith site.

80 Two men with an anthropomorphic fish. The unpainted neck of the smaller man shows that the ropes go in front of him, and his size indicates his distance. Two different types of perspective are thus used.

81 This Classic hunting scene shows a bear and two cubs trapped in a den. One arrow is imbedded in the adult bear. Two have missed and are in the den wall. The den is in front of the hunter, because his foot is hidden by it.

82 Hopi consultants saw this scene as stages in the transformation between man (on the left) and animal (on the right). They felt this may have reflected Puebloan ideas about the relationship between man and animal.

83 This Classic Mimbres bowl
shows a woman carrying a basket
filled with wood, a man carrying a
log, and a dog. Perspective is shown
by placing the woman's arm in front
of the body. The small size of the
male figure may signify that he is in
the background.

84 This woman's sash was found in
the Anasazi area to the north of the
Mimbres area. Hanging from the
upper woven section are 241 yucca
fiber strings. Identical textiles appear
to be depicted on women in Mimbres
bowls such as that in plate 85. The
sash was apparently passed between
the legs and held up by a separate
belt.

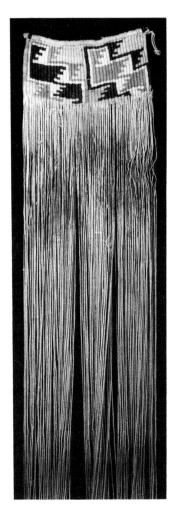

85 A Classic Mimbres bowl, with one woman carrying a basket,
and another a baby. The women wear sashes (like that in plate 84)
and belts.

Several other bowl scenes were read in a similar way. Puebloan religion stresses the oneness of man and other living beings; man is one small part of the natural order; all living beings, not just man, are embodied by spirits. The Hopi wondered whether the men being 'eaten' by the fish was actually the depiction of the man-like spirit of the fish changing from its fish state to its human-like state. Such an interpretation fits with Puebloan cosmology and may well have been shared by the Mimbres people. Perhaps the most convincing depiction of this transformation concept shows an animal similar   plate 82 to a dog on one portion of the bowl, a form which is half animal and half man next to it, and then a man in a similar posture to the others. This image can be understood as the transformation from animal to man. The Hopi felt that many examples of this art fit within their oral history, mythology, and world view.

Interpretations of this kind, combined with the depiction of mythic creatures and imaginary scenes, suggest that some of the Mimbres figurative bowls were used to portray religious events and symbolism. This is not surprising given the complex blending of everyday life and religion among the modern day Puebloan people.

Turning from the difficult problem of interpreting the images, we have discovered some interesting aspects of the artistic canons themselves. Based on arguments first advanced by our Hopi consultants, it appears that some Mimbres artists were using perspective in their bowl paintings. In a number of examples there are attempts to differentiate between foreground and background. This was accomplished in several ways. One method was to outline legs or other body parts or objects to separate these from objects which   plates 76, 80, 85 lay behind them. Another method was to mask part of one object or figure by   plate 83 another which lay in front of it. A fine example is the hiding of a dog's feet by its tail, thereby showing that the tail was in the foreground and lay in front of its feet. A last method is more difficult to demonstrate conclusively, even though it is similar to our own conventions. The foreground objects were depicted larger than their counterparts in the background. An excellent   plate 70 example of this method is the bullroarer – a small wooden object about 10 to   plate XIV 13 cm long, frequently decorated with feathers, and so on – shown almost as large as a man. Today these are twirled on a string so that they make a roaring sound during various ceremonies in the modern pueblos. The exaggerated size of the bullroarer is probably an attempt to place it in the foreground, while the man twirling it is in the background.

Of all the Mimbres imagery perhaps the most unexpected is the use of imagery reversal. While a number of examples exist, the bowl showing 'ghost' and bird forms in positive and negative respectively is a superb example.   plate 72 Another vessel shows a crane and a floating human head; the head and the legs   plate V of the crane are shown in negative. This latter bowl was found in the 400s room block on the Mattocks site.

In considering these rather sophisticated aspects of Mimbres art, one is confronted with the question of who painted the bowls. Were they men or women, or did both make pottery? Were there a few specialists, or was this an activity undertaken by every household? The answers to these questions would shed light on the production of Mimbres ceramics, on the way in which the vessels were used, and potentially on Mimbres society itself. Disappointingly few answers have so far been found.

Today Puebloan women make and paint their own pottery. Whether this was also true for the Mimbres is unknown. On the other hand, we do have some ideas about how many people may have produced these bowls. One must realize that the total number produced is very large. Sites like the Mattocks ruin contain tens of thousands of sherds from painted bowls. These were used and broken and were never buried in a grave. It appears that at any one time a typical household would have possessed a number which were probably used to serve food. The typical bowl probably lasted only a few years before it was accidentally broken, so every family would have used several over a period of time. Inspection of the sherds themselves, however, shows a paucity of figurative elements. While some figurative bowls were used in the household, a disproportionate number were used as mortuary goods. It seems likely that many households produced painted pottery for domestic purposes, and these were usually painted with geometric designs. At the same time, a few artists may well have produced most of the vessels ultimately used as funerary offerings, and these painters may have produced most of the figurative scenes and complex geometric designs.

Several facts support such a pattern of Mimbres painted ceramic production. There are some interesting differences between the bowls found at the largest Mimbres villages and those from other sites. All settlements have some painted vessels, but the smaller villages, both those near the major ones and those in peripheral areas, have fewer well-executed bowls; most pots are much inferior to those from the large sites. It is very seldom that well-executed figurative bowls are encountered at small ones. At one such site, several high-quality bowls were found nested inside each other on the floor of a room. Perhaps these were trade goods, imported from a large pueblo in the Mimbres Valley and placed inside each other to save space during transport.

The most reasonable explanation for this pattern is that most bowls of high quality were produced in the larger pueblos. They would then have been traded out to smaller villages, where, in all likelihood, simpler painted bowls were produced for local use. Figurative motifs were rarely used and the quality of work is not outstanding. Apparently, few bowls were used at the smallest sites. These were probably seasonally occupied and it is likely that no bowls were produced there. Thus, there may have been a dual system of bowl production, with many members of the society making some painted bowls but only a few individuals being responsible for the best-quality work. These exceptional products would often have been used as grave goods and widely traded within the Mimbres culture area.

The possibility that some potters were full- or part-time specialists is suggested by the idea that such sensitive artists would have had to paint bowls regularly to keep up their skills. It is easy to imagine that a single potter could produce 100 or more vessels in a year. In a 20-year productive span, a single potter could make 2000 pots. Based on the number of sites and their size, we estimate that no more than 15,000 to 20,000 bowls were used as funerary offerings during the Classic period, although many more bowls than this were made. Following such a line of reasoning, 10 potters would have been able to produce *all* the funerary vessels for the entire 150-year span of the Classic Mimbres period. While there is no definite evidence that only two or three painters per generation were responsible for these bowls, our understanding of ceramic production from ethnographic data suggests that a handful of potters may have been responsible for most of the great Mimbres bowls. Thus the 'sword' motif may be so consistently rendered because all of these were painted by a single potter, and the same applies for the image-reversal bowls.

Our conclusions about Mimbres pottery, therefore, are as follows. The design style evolved increasingly rapidly until sometime in the AD 1000s when it seemed to explode in a display of innovation and variety. There were few outside stimula for this phenomenon, and it may well have been the work of a handful of potters. The bowls depict many everyday objects and scenes, but are also frequently religious in character. This is not surprising given the probability that Mimbres daily life and religion would have been closely interwoven. We have no evidence that the depiction on a bowl was used to signify the social position of the deceased with whom it was buried. The status and fame of the potter may instead have been an important consideration in determining which bowl was placed with which individual, the bowls of a well-known and respected full-time specialist possibly being interred with the important members of the community. Such a usage would parallel today's use of art, where the owner of a Picasso receives acclaim and status, or uses the painting to attract it, regardless of the subject matter of his painting. We should not be surprised if the Mimbres also had a sophisticated appreciation and use of their art form.

11 Classic Mimbres society

Architecture and painted pottery provide us with our best information on Mimbres society, but by no means all. A number of other types of evidence help us reconstruct quite a bit about Mimbres daily life, their trade networks, and other aspects of their material culture.

Life in the villages centered around food procurement. Fields had to be cleared, and crops planted, weeded, and harvested. The staple crop, maize, which probably provided about half their caloric intake, required grinding before eating. This grinding was most likely done by the women, and probably lasted several hours each day. Besides farming, the men must have spent considerable time out hunting and in preparing for it. The bowls depict men using bows and arrows and snares. Some bowls may depict nets, examples of which have been found in dry caves in the Southwest. The nets were probably used in communal hunts where rabbits were driven into them and caught. Not only did the Mimbres devote considerable time and energy to food procurement, they were becoming less and less efficient at it. This is a topic taken up in detail in chapter 12 (pp. 149–57).

plate 81

The annual cycle was almost certainly marked by various religious and secular ceremonial events, with different rituals inaugurating each season. Analogy with the modern Pueblo Indians suggests that most ceremonial activity would have taken place during the growing season, when the need for rain was a major concern. Once crops had been harvested and stored, house construction and various maintenance activities were undertaken. This was probably a relatively slack time. Gambling, which is possibly depicted in bowl paintings, may have provided recreation. This was also likely to have been a time for producing decorative or non-utilitarian items, and for sending trading parties to other villages in the Mimbres area and beyond.

Mimbres artistic activity was heavily focused on the production of painted bowls, but a wide range of other goods was made as well. Only some of these items were durable enough to have been preserved in archaeological deposits, but the depictions we find on the bowls help fill out the repertoire of Mimbres artifacts. We can see from the human figures on the bowls that jewelry was frequently worn, and a wide variety of this has been found in archaeological deposits. Arm bands worn on the biceps are frequently depicted on males, but they must have been perishable, because nothing resembling them has been recovered. Shell bracelets worn on the lower arm have been found, however.

plates XV, 78

Sometimes four or five bracelets were worn on one arm. The shells were cut from a large marine clam. They are always found in a completely finished form and must have been imported from the Gulf of California as a finished product, probably via the Hohokam of Arizona.

Turquoise was used to make several kinds of ornament. Most frequently it was made into beads. They were sometimes strung singly, but were also frequently combined with other beads, made of either shell or stone. Larger pieces of turquoise were made into pendants, which were generally oblong with a hole drilled at one end. They are sometimes found as matched pairs and may have been used as earrings; however, none of the males or females shown on the bowls wear anything like earrings. A few pendants made out of other stones were also found. These are frequently in the form of effigies of various animals.

plate III

plate 31

We have more indirect evidence of other forms of body adornment and clothing. Men's faces are frequently depicted on the bowls with broad markings, suggesting the use of body paint. Stone palettes have been found with traces of paint on them that may have been used in the preparation of body coloring. Several locally available minerals were ground up to be used as paint. Hematite produced red and yellow, while ground malachite, a turquoise-related mineral, gave a blue-green color. Such pigment, of course, was used for more than body paint. Deposits in dry caves have produced wooden prayer sticks and other perishable artifacts painted in these colors.

Even though we have a large number of bowl paintings of people, the style of Mimbres dress is not clear. Masks and various animal costumes are frequently shown. Based on analogies with the modern Pueblo Indians these may represent ceremonial paraphernalia. Women frequently wear some form of belt and sash. We can see from the bowl paintings that the belts were tied at the front with a bow, and the sash was of a cord-like material. We know that these were two distinct items of clothing, because some paintings show them removed and lying as separate pieces. Elsewhere in the Southwest, garments fitting this description have been found. The belts are of braided human hair and the sashes of yucca fiber. The sashes are neatly woven for 60 cm of their length, with long fringes left unwoven for another 60 cm. The woven part was worn between the legs as a loin cloth, and the fringe hung down at the back below the waist.[32] At least one Mimbres burial contained yucca fiber material that was very likely the remains of such a sash.[33] Bowls also show the use of sandals, and some examples made of yucca fiber have been found in dry caves; people are also depicted with bare feet.

plates 78, 83, 85

plate 84

Objects which appear to be blankets are shown in a few bowl scenes. We have recovered both charred cotton cloth and charred cotton seeds from various Mimbres sites. Today cotton is grown in the desert area along the lower Mimbres River, and we think that its cultivation would have been restricted to the lower part of the Mimbres region prehistorically. It is likely that cotton, cotton fabric, and garments were important trade items. Bone weaving tools are frequently found on Mimbres sites. The blankets depicted on the bowls have quite elaborate designs, but we have no knowledge of the repertoire of designs that was used, nor whether they approached the complexity we find in the bowl paintings. Unfortunately, no examples of Mimbres weaving have survived. Interestingly, no bowls show people wearing winter clothing. Temperatures commonly drop below freezing and snow often falls, so the Mimbres must have had winter clothing. To judge by the historic Pueblo Indians, blankets and blanket-like dresses would have been worn, as well as rabbit-skin cloaks.

plates 78, 83   Besides blankets, the Mimbres wove baskets, and these must have been important for carrying harvested crops and for transporting food and other items along trade routes. A number of bowls clearly depict large carrying baskets. These are shown being carried on the back with a rope or belt passed across the forehead. The baskets are always depicted with geometric designs, but, as is the case for textiles, no definite Mimbres baskets have survived.

plate 28   Several other kinds of object have also been recovered. Several carved stone items were probably used in ceremonial activities; these include a large frog carved from a piece of turquoise, and several stone bowls with human-like figures carved in low relief. The Mimbres also manufactured enigmatic stone plate 26   objects which are frequently called hoes. These were shaped from flat pieces of stone, using a chipping process. They range from 10 cm to 33 cm in length and are always slightly tapered at one end. They are frequently found in caches containing up to forty-seven hoes. Their function remains a mystery. None has ever been found that shows clear signs or wear or use; moreover, no bowl depicts any such object. They may, nevertheless, have served as hoes; the Mimbres must have had some tool for digging and cleaning irrigation canals. On the other hand, they really do look something like artifacts found elsewhere in the Southwest that are thought to be agave knives. The agave, or century plant, has thick fleshy leaves which can be cut and roasted. The plant grows in the Mimbres area, but we have never found a pit used to roast them.

plate 24   Arrowheads and knives were chipped from stone as well as from obsidian or volcanic glass imported into the Mimbres Valley. Bone tools were used for plate 25   chipping stone, and as punches or awls. Occasionally these were decorated, but for the most part they were simple utilitarian items.

The inhabitants of any one village were capable of producing almost all the goods they needed, but they did trade for some necessities and useful articles. More of their trade, however, was devoted to exotic, non-utilitarian artifacts and materials which, although they were not essential in the strict sense, must have served important sociological functions. Foreign-made pottery and shell plate 29   artifacts are examples of such non-essential goods. The nature of Mimbres trade changed considerably over time, with respect both to how much trade there was and to with whom they traded.

As we have seen, there is little evidence for trade during the Early Pithouse period. Major inter-regional trade began during the Late Pithouse period, when the Mimbres traded with various immediately adjacent groups and with the Hohokam further away in central Arizona. Non-perishable items were probably traded in both directions. The Mimbres exchanged their own painted vessels for foreign pottery and shell objects.

During the Classic period, trade with the Hohokam greatly diminished; only shell ornaments continued to be brought into the Mimbres area in quantities. Also at this time there was much less movement of ceramics either into or out of the region. While these relationships were diminishing, trade with more distant zones to the north and south seems to have markedly increased. The Mimbres seem to have begun participating in a large trade network that linked the Southwest and at least the northern periphery of Mesoamerica.

Several exotic items were being imported from Mexico, for example parrots or macaws. Several have been found buried in Mimbres sites. There is no evidence they were ever eaten. Parrot bones are not found in refuse middens, house-floor deposits, or hearths. Today, brightly colored parrot feathers are vital religious items for Pueblo Indians. Mimbres bowls depict parrots in several different contexts, showing that both the bird and its feathers were probably important in the ceremonial life of the prehistoric communities. No feathers have survived, of course, and the burials uncovered to date by archaeological work probably under-represent the number of parrots and quantities of feathers that were imported.

The other exotic import from Mexico was copper bells. These were similar   plate 30
to sleigh bells with a cross-shaped opening, and were cast by the lost-wax process. Interestingly, large copper mines still exist in the Mimbres area, where native nuggets or slabs are found even today. Yet no copper artifacts, either in raw or processed form, have been found in Mimbres sites except for these imported bells. They are quite rare in Mimbres sites, with only about twenty-five known examples, all from Classic period deposits. They were even more rarely used as funerary goods, suggesting that they were quite valuable.

There is some thought among archaeologists that these items represent more than just trade, and that new religious beliefs or gods were introduced along with their ceremonial paraphernalia. The study of this interesting phenomenon is still in its infancy, but various scholars see elements of a new religious complex reflected in the figurative depictions of Classic Mimbres bowls.

A number of perishable items could have been traded to the south in exchange for the parrots, copper bells, and other goods. These may have included cotton textiles and buffalo hides from the plains. Perhaps the most important item, and certainly one for which we have the best archaeological evidence, is turquoise. This blue-green stone continues to be important among the Pueblo Indians today. It is exchanged among the villages and is used in ceremonial activities. Some turquoise from the Southwest reached Mesoamerica in the prehistoric period, and it has even been suggested that it was traded as far south as the Mayan area of the Yucatan. Turquoise was mined prehistorically well to the north of the Mimbres area.

Where the Mimbres found their turquoise is still a subject of debate. There are still mines in the Mimbres area that produce or have produced turquoise. Yet, with only one possible exception, we find no evidence that the Mimbres ever mined these deposits or produced any turquoise artifacts themselves. Only finished pieces have been found, suggesting that the Mimbres were part of a major north-south trading network starting in northern New Mexico and going south to Mesoamerica. The Mimbres seemingly acquired goods by serving as middlemen. While most of the turquoise produced in the north would have passed through the Mimbres on its way to the south, small quantities may have been kept. Conversely, most of the parrots and copper bells from the south may have been carried on into the northern Anasazi area with only some items remaining behind.

In contrast to the relatively stable external trade, there was a marked increase during the Classic period in the trade within the Mimbres region, and even within the Mimbres Valley itself. Much of the intra-regional trade probably consisted of perishable goods. Cotton may again have been important, being moved from lower elevations where it was grown, to villages at higher elevations. The distances are not great, so food could have been traded extensively. Meat and piñon nuts were the most likely foods to be transported.

While evidence for trade in these foods has not survived in archaeological deposits, we do have evidence for the movement of a number of non-perishable items. These include obsidian, ground stone axes, pottery, and miscellaneous minerals such as malachite and quartz crystals. Obsidian, or volcanic glass, was used for arrowheads and cutting tools. There are several deposits on the periphery of the Mimbres area, and it was traded from these locations throughout the region. Stone axes, probably used for felling and shaping construction timbers rather than for securing firewood, were ground from a hard stone, a pre-Cambrian granite which is available only in a few restricted localities. One outcrop of this stone is near the Galaz site, and it is likely that the Galaz population manufactured axes from this stone and traded them to other villages throughout the region.

plate 27

fig. 26, plate 34

By the Classic Mimbres period, the culinary and storage jars had attained considerable size. The average Classic utilitarian jar was about 36 cm high and could hold about 19 liters. Fragments of jars have been found which were 60 cm high and held over 80 liters. Such jars were quite common and more than half of the pottery fragments we recovered came from them.

Rock inclusions were added as temper to the clay, to improve its strength and firing qualities. During the Late Pithouse period the tempering material used in the smaller jars was common stream sand that could be locally obtained. When studies were conducted on the temper of the Classic period utility jars, we found a completely unexpected pattern. The people who lived

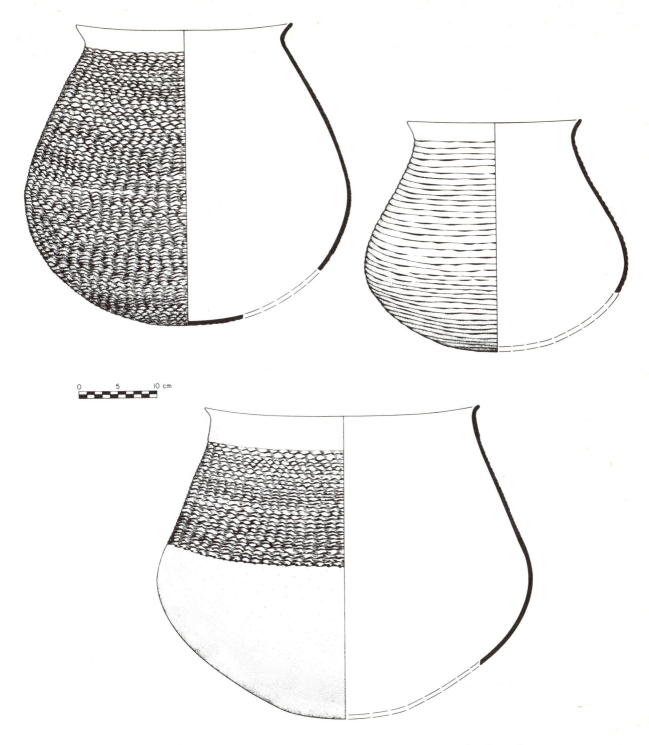

26 Utility jars of the Classic period. Corrugated exteriors became universal and very large storage jars were produced.

in the southern part of the Mimbres Valley appeared to be going out of the valley to collect a particular type of granitic material to use as temper. But they used this only for their cooking and storage jars and never for painted bowls. It was not available anywhere in the Mimbres Valley, yet we have found utility jars made with it throughout the valley, including at the Mattocks and Galaz sites. In fact, something over one-fifth of all the large jars at these sites were made with this granite temper.

This information presents us with a typical archaeological dilemma. It seems very unlikely that the potters at the Galaz and Mattocks sites were traveling the 20 to 25 miles to obtain the temper for themselves. Is it possible that they obtained it through trade? Is it perhaps also possible that jars made with this special temper were considered so superior that they were carried up the valley as trade goods? Or was there something that was being traded in these jars, so that they were, so to speak, merely the tin cans, and not the object of trade at all?

We do have some answers to these questions. It is unlikely that the jars were no more than dispensable containers. The Mimbres had large carrying baskets, which would have been lighter and less breakable than the jars, and better for transporting all goods except liquids. We can think of no liquid that the Mimbres would have needed to carry those distances. The most likely explanation for the distribution of the jars throughout the valley is that the granitic temper improved their durablilty. We have conducted tests to compare those made with granitic temper and those with the regular river-sand temper, in order to consider this possibility. So far we have found no difference in the strength or durability of the pottery, but we still believe this to be the likely explanation.

Regardless of the factors underlying the movement of these large heavy jars throughout the valley, their distribution does suggest that trade and the movement of people were common in the Mimbres area. We should not find this surprising. The similarities in architecture, ceremonial structures, and artifacts, like pottery, all suggest that the Mimbres were in frequent contact with each other and that groups did not live in total isolation from each other.

During most of the prehistory of the Southwest there was little distinction of status between the people of different villages or even between individuals within single villages. This is not surprising, because for most of human history differences in individual status has been relatively minor, mostly based on individual achievement rather than on inherited position. Only when population densities rise in certain regions do we see some form of complex organization developing. Then status differentiation emerges, as positions associated with particular kin groups stimulate the need for status markers or elite goods.

The prehistoric Southwest with its arid environment and generally low population density is not a likely place to find such inherited status roles. Instead we find that status was an individual and ephemeral phenomenon.

One exceptional individual could obtain a considerable degree of status and authority during his lifetime, but it would not be passed on to his descendants. Through social institutions, such as religious and civil offices, wealth was attracted away from those individuals and households who had more, to those who had less, diminishing the concentration of wealth and differences in status.[34]

There were, however, times when marked differentiation in status did develop. One important case where evidence for social stratification exists is at Chaco Canyon in the Anasazi area. Here was a social system that was contemporary with the Classic Mimbres, and which incorporated social ranking. Did such a structure also exist for the Classic Mimbres?

The answer to this question is far from clear; we have various strands of evidence but they appear to be conflicting. One problem is the relationship between the various types of community. We have seen that there were several different sizes and classes of Classic Mimbres site. There were roughly twenty large villages in the valley and elsewhere in the greater Mimbres area. Those villages are distinct from the rest of the Classic Mimbres sites in a number of ways. Not only were they considerably larger than the others, but they have yielded most of the turquoise and other exotic finds from the Mimbres area, including all the known examples of parrots and copper bells. Of these sites, the Galaz and perhaps a couple of others seemed to have a disproportionate share of these exotic goods.

In sharp contrast to these few large villages were the smaller ones of less than twenty-five rooms. We have already discussed how these were frequently located in relatively marginal areas, and how the smallest of them were probably not permanently occupied. Besides their dimensions, there are differences in the material remains found at each type of site. The smaller sites contain few exotic goods, such as turquoise, and many fewer well-executed bowls and imported ceramics. They also show that less energy was invested in building ceremonial structures.

Some of these differences can be attributed to the smaller size of the communities, but surely not all. Maybe the occupants were simply poorer – at least in terms of non-utilitarian goods – than the people at the larger sites. Such differences are one line of evidence indicating that high-status individuals lived at the larger communities.

Our attempts to find direct evidence of their presence, however, have been unsuccessful. We would expect such an elite to reside in rooms larger and more elaborate than the average, but we have no evidence at all for such structures. We would also expect individuals to be buried in more elaborate graves, or with greater quantities of grave goods, than the remainder of the population. We have found a few elaborate graves with rock linings. Others have larger quantities of grave goods – a child burial at the Galaz site had twenty ceramic vessels as funerary offerings. But we have not found elaborately constructed graves which also contained great quantities of grave offerings. Indeed, more elaborate graves and the simpler burials with unusual numbers of grave goods are neither located near each other in one district, nor are they in prominent places within the villages.

Despite these few suggestions of an elite, and of possible craft specialists who produced the best painted bowls, we really do not have convincing evidence of true status differentiation among the Classic Mimbres. It may be that such a pattern was just emerging, and that not all the associated physical manifestations of an elite had developed by the time the Mimbres culture disappeared. In all probability the Mimbres were an essentially egalitarian people with an incipient form of elite beginning to emerge at a few villages like the Galaz site. This was reflected in only limited ways in the remains of the Mimbres culture.

12 Mimbres subsistence

We put a great deal of effort into understanding how the Mimbres people made a living as farmers, collectors of wild plants, and hunters.[35] In the process of screening the excavated soil, we recovered a large number of animal bones, providing evidence for hunting activities. Screening recovered a few charred remains of plants, but to retrieve better data on plant use required more specialized techniques. One important procedure was the use of a method involving flotation. This fairly recent archaeological innovation works on the principle that carbonized organic material floats. Samples of soil from hearths, ash lenses, and any other areas likely to contain charred plant remains, were placed in a tank of water. Small pieces of charcoal and other carbonized material floated to the surface, where they were skimmed off using a very fine mesh strainer. This technique recovered seeds and charcoal which provided accurate information on all aspects of plant use.

Another process for recovering evidence of plant use is pollen analysis. Samples of soil can be removed from the floors of rooms and even the surfaces of grinding stones, taking care to reduce the contamination of these samples by modern pollen. All ancient pollen spores were then extracted from the soil samples by a complex chemical process. The spores of different species and genera of plants are of different sizes and shapes, so can be distinguished under a high-powered microscope. This meticulous and time-consuming process has produced important information on Mimbres diet and also on plants that grew in the region at various times.

But we learned far more than just what plants and animals the Mimbres ate and used. We could identify the proportions in which they used the various resources available to them. We were particularly interested in the staples of their diet, and if there were changes in their diet during their history. Did the Mimbres diet change from wild foods to domesticated plants? Did they begin to hunt different animals? Most importantly, did the Mimbres ever have trouble obtaining an adequate food supply, such as periods of famine? And, perhaps most interestingly, did an inadequate food supply contribute to the disappearance of the Mimbres people?

Interpreting plant and animal remains from archaeological sites is far from straightforward. How does one interpret the presence of a lot of deer bones, but few rabbit bones on a site? One's initial·reaction is that the people who lived in the village ate mostly deer. But the predominance of deer bones could simply be due to the fact that the smaller and more fragile rabbit bones decompose more easily and are destroyed by dogs and other scavengers, so do not survive. Again, the charred seeds of wild grass found in a hearth may not represent the use of the seeds for food so much as the use of grass to kindle a fire.

No method of analysis completely surmounts these and other difficulties in interpreting archaeological remains. But there are ways of avoiding some major pitfalls. The method we used involved making comparisons between sites. By searching for changes in plant and animal use between sites of different periods and in different locations in the valley, we could determine if different food-procurement strategies were being employed. For example, we can assume that the processes that destroyed rabbit bones were reasonably constant for all periods in the valley, so if we find an increase in the amount of rabbit bone from one period to another we can be reasonably sure that a change in hunting practices occurred. Similarly, if we see a sudden increase in the amount of wild grass seeds in hearths, this most probably represents a change in eating habits, rather than a new way of kindling fire. Of course, such an approach does not allow us to estimate how much rabbit meat or how much grass seed was being consumed; we can find changes in the use of each resource individually, but not make absolute estimates of its use. Nor can we make accurate comparisons between different types of resources, because of the problems of differential preservation.

With this procedure in mind we began collecting samples from the Early and Late Pithouse period sites, the Classic Mimbres villages, as well as from sites of the two post-Mimbres occupations in the valley. We quickly saw that very substantial changes took place in hunting practices and in the use of plants. This was particularly obvious when we compared the Classic Mimbres period sites with either the earlier or later ones. This will be discussed further on.

Our new data could not explain precisely what caused these changes in resource use, although there are two likely reasons. Either the population density in the valley changed, obliging the people to adopt new food-procurement strategies, or the climate altered, resulting in modifications to the wild resources and also the ability to cultivate plants. To discover the factors that accompanied these changes in food consumption we needed to find out if either the population density or the climate changed, or both.

It proved impossible to estimate how many people lived in the valley during each period. It was simply beyond our resources to locate all the sites in the Mimbres Valley and the immediately surrounding zones. So we devised a plan to sample the entire area. We first found and recorded all the sites in selected parts of the territory. This information was used to estimate the total number of sites for the area as a whole. The survey was accomplished by a crew of between 3 and 5 individuals; they walked over the land, spaced 10 to 15 m apart, looking carefully for any signs of prehistoric remains. This time-consuming process was the only way to produce good population estimates.

We ultimately conducted site surveys over 90 sq miles of the valley and surrounding area, and located over 500 sites. This number, however, could not tell us the number of people who lived there at any given time. First of all, not all the sites were permanent residential communities; many were just places where some limited activity was performed, for example a hunting station where hunters repaired some of their tools. Our first step was to determine which of them were actually habitation sites. We did this by comparing the surface artifacts and architectural features seen at the surveyed sites with the remains at the sites we had excavated. Because we had excavated on both permanent habitation sites and sites used for occasional activities, we could determine which types of site we found on survey. We were also able to date most of the surveyed sites, by comparing their pottery and architecture with those at excavated sites.

We next needed to estimate the number of people that lived on each habitation site, which varied considerably in size. A village with two pithouses could not have had the same number of people as the Classic pueblo at the Galaz site. To deal with these variations, the actual amount of space that had been roofed on each site was estimated. Even though the architecture changed over time, the amount of roofed space used by each person probably stayed reasonably constant.

Two final adjustments were necessary, to reflect the abandonment of houses and any variation in the duration of our time periods. If a typical house lasted fifty years before it fell into disuse, then during a period of a hundred years, only half the standing houses would be in use at any one time. Similarly, if historical periods were of different lengths, more houses would have been built during the longer periods than the shorter ones, even though their populations might have been equal at any one time. So we needed to adjust our figures according to how long houses lasted and how long the different time periods were. The information which enabled these adjustments to be made came from our excavations. So our population estimates were based on data from both site surveys and excavations.

Using the procedure discussed above, we can estimate the relative numbers of people in the valley at different times, just by comparing the total roofed area adjusted appropriately. Finally, to estimate the absolute or actual number of people, we need to know how much roofed area each person used. We have employed information on the per capita roofed area of the historic Pueblo Indians to make this conversion from relative to absolute population estimates.

Our conclusions about the relative population sizes for different periods show substantial changes through time. The population during the Early Pithouse period was quite small compared with the later periods. In absolute terms, it may have been only about 500 people. Subsequently, the Late Pithouse period witnessed a substantial growth in population, and by the late AD 800s or early 900s there were about $2\frac{1}{2}$ times as many people in the valley as   *fig. 27*

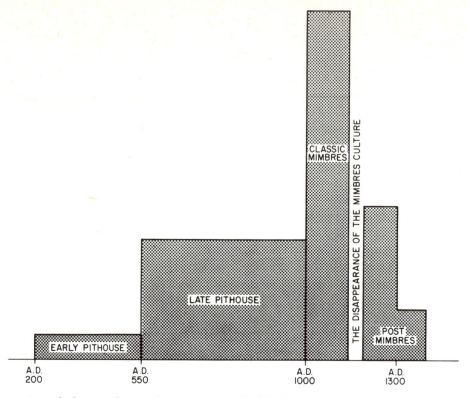

27 *A graph showing the population growth in the Mimbres valley. When the population peaked in the Classic Mimbres period, it was some fourteen times greater than that of* AD *200. There was a marked drop in the post-Mimbres period, and after* AD *1400 the valley was abandoned.*

during the Early Pithouse period – amounting to about 1250 individuals. The population continued to grow, and reached a peak during the Classic Mimbres period with over $7\frac{1}{2}$ times as many people as during the earliest period. There were then roughly 3500 or 4000 people. After the disappearance of the Mimbres culture, the occupation of the valley dropped to only half that of the Classic period. Later still, the population of the AD 1400s was even smaller, and only slightly larger than that of the Early Pithouse period.

We can see that the population rose steadily for some 900 years during the Mimbres occupation, and then went into a decline for 300 years until the valley was finally abandoned completely around AD 1450. Was the very large Classic Mimbres population too large to be sustained by the resources of the valley? Were new techniques for precuring resources introduced at this time of maximum population? Finally, did population growth play a significant role in the eventual disappearance of the Mimbres? While we cannot fully answer these questions, we do have some partial answers.

All our evidence indicates that the increased population of the Classic Mimbres period necessitated considerable adjustments in the food-procurement strategy. Some important signs of this came from our site survey.

During the Early Pithouse period, sites were located in the optimal farming areas along the floodplain of the Mimbres River. The early occupants of the valley certainly made use of the desert and mountain areas, but rarely built permanent villages there.

Sometime in the Late Pithouse period, however, this pattern began to change, and settlements were occasionally located in more marginal areas. Small pithouse villages begin to be found in the higher more mountainous zones as well as in the desert. A major change in the distribution of villages did not occur until the Classic period. Then, large numbers of sites were located in marginal areas, both in the mountains and the deserts. In fact, just about every piece of cultivatable land has a small Classic Mimbres period site in the vicinity. These were sometimes quite small, having only a room or two. Since their construction was not substantial, it is our belief that many of these sites were used only on a seasonal basis, serving as residences during the farming season and as places to store equipment and crops. The people who used them probably took the foodstuffs and tools back to the larger villages for the winter.

Small sites are occasionally associated with agricultural terraces or dams. *fig. 28* The dam builders would select a small tributary of the Mimbres River and lay

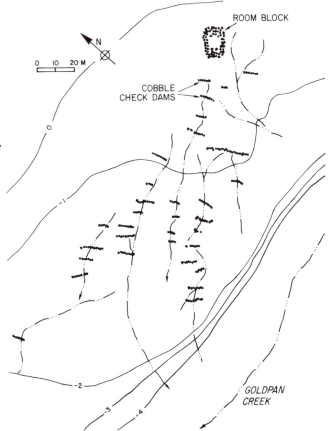

28 Small dam-systems were located on the headwaters of tributaries to the Mimbres River. Since these increase agricultural production, they prove there was a shortage of arable land during the population peak of the Classic Mimbres period.

a single row of stones end to end across the drainage. The dams were 6 to 12 m apart. Up to 50 or 60 were built along less than a mile of the tributary, and would slow rain runoff, collecting the moisture and silt behind them. The net result was that crops had better growing conditions than otherwise, and many areas became fertile that would otherwise have been unproductive. While these dams are minor constructions in comparison with the extensive terrace and irrigation systems built by other prehistoric peoples such as the Inca, they nevertheless required effort and inventiveness, and show how the need for more farmland was brought on by the increased population of the Classic Mimbres period. Such dams are almost always associated with small pueblos of the Classic Mimbres period and are rarely found at any other sites.

Besides these activities in the outlying marginal areas, new farming strategies were adopted in the main valley. At some point, the Mimbres must have begun to employ irrigation agriculture. Today the valley is farmed using many small, gravity-fed irrigation ditches. These are only a meter or so wide and most of them run a mile or less. The methods employed in building and maintaining them are completely within the capabilities of the prehistoric Mimbres. In fact, we suspect that some or even most of the irrigation ditches in use today were first built in prehistoric times.

Unfortunately, it is very hard to date an irrigation canal, and we have been unable to prove that the prehistoric Mimbres built any that are currently in use. We do, however, have some indirect evidence for irrigation during the Classic period. First of all, we know that the Mimbres were aware of such techniques. Both the Anasazi and the Hohokam had evolved systems by this same time and we have seen that the Mimbres were in contact with both areas.

Equally, we believe the Classic Mimbres must have been using irrigation agriculture simply in order to survive. We have estimated how much farmland the Mimbres had, and the quantities of wild plant and animal food available to them. We can also estimate how much food they could have grown both with and without irrigation, using information from historic Pueblo Indian farming techniques. It seems that the Classic Mimbres people would not have been able to get enough food to survive unless they had employed irrigation. Collecting wild plants, hunting, and farming without irrigation would have been inadequate.

We can see from the site survey that population growth in the Mimbres Valley had a considerable impact on the location of new settlements and on the developing of new farming techniques. But there were several other inter-related effects, both on the environment itself and on the Mimbres lifestyle.

The people began to alter their environment to a considerable degree. Their most notable impact was on the vegetation in the river floodplain. During the earlier periods, when the human population was small, the trees of the floodplain – cottonwoods, alders, and other water-loving trees – served as a major source of firewood and construction timber. This is indicated by the charred fragments of beams recovered in archaeological excavations. That these species were also used for firewood has been demonstrated by the study of charcoal recovered from hearths by flotation.

As the population grew, trees along the river were progressively reduced in number. By the height of the Classic Mimbres period it seems that the river bottom was almost denuded of large trees; to such an extent that trees and shrubs on hillslopes away from the river had to be used for firewood and house construction. We presume that during this period the floodplain was covered with irrigated fields, so people must have traveled progressively greater distances in order to obtain both firewood for heating and cooking, and the timbers used to construct new houses. As the trees were felled, large areas in the floodplain and around settlements were being disturbed by farming. Areas that had previously been covered by grasses and shrubs were colonized by weeds – to judge by the increase in weed seeds recovered by flotation and in weed pollen found in samples dating to the Classic period.

Concurrent with the changes in vegetation came fluctuations in some animal numbers. When the human population in the valley was low and the riverine vegetation still undisturbed, it was a prime habitat for the small cottontail rabbit. But as these areas were cleared for farming and sown, and fallow fields took up most of the floodplain, the habitat became much more favorable for the larger jackrabbit. Accordingly, we find a preponderance of cottontail rabbit bones in the sites from the earlier periods when the population was small, and an increase in jackrabbit bones at sites of the Classic Mimbres period when the population reached its peak.

Along with this shift in the types of rabbits, we see an overall change in hunting patterns. Throughout the prehistoric occupation, deer and rabbits were the staple sources of meat, even though many other animals were hunted. When the human population was small, more deer than rabbits were hunted and consumed. Yet, as the population increased, reaching a peak in the Classic period, rabbits became more common than deer.

This shift indicates a change in hunting patterns. A single deer obviously provides much more meat than a single rabbit, so one would obviously rather hunt deer than rabbits, if one had a reasonable chance of success. As the human population rose, the rate at which deer were caught also increased, so that they became relatively more scarce and progressively harder to hunt successfully. At the same time, the clearing of fields for farming had produced a new habitat suitable especially for jackrabbits. Not only were these rabbits hunted because they were more plentiful and available, but they were probably a serious pest, consuming valuable crops. Hunting them not only provided meat, but also helped reduce crop loss.

Despite substantial changes in natural vegetation and the wild animal population, the vegetable diet of the Mimbres probably did not vary much over this entire time span. Maize remained the staple crop regardless of the population density. There were also only minor changes in the use of wild plants such as cactus fruit, grass seeds, and cattail heads. As the population grew the need for more food was met by both more intensive farming and more intensive collecting of wild resources. One class of food was not abandoned at the expense of others, and the proportions obtained by farming and by collecting remained relatively constant.

The ability of the Mimbres to provision themselves adequately was affected by changes not only in their numbers but also in their environment. It is clear that there were no major shifts in the climate during this time span. Nevertheless, we must remember that those who lived in the Mimbres area led a tenuous existence, and even small changes in the rainfall or temperature could have serious consequences.

Our best information on rainfall comes from tree-ring samples. The width of tree ring gives a good although not perfect estimate of the amount of rainfall in any one year. Wide rings are grown when there was ample rainfall and narrow rings during droughts. Unfortunately we do not yet have a complete year-by-year tree-ring sequence for the prehistoric period in the Mimbres Valley. Some periods are covered by samples that are too small to use or by specimens from undatable trees, leaving many gaps in our series. But archaeologists working a little further north on the Mogollon region have been more fortunate, and a good rainfall sequence based on tree rings is available from these.[36] This prehistoric sequence shows that there was considerable variability from year to year, but it contains no indication of a long catastrophic drought. While crops may have failed in a number of years, these were generally followed by good years. The extensive storage areas in Classic Mimbres pueblos indicate that the storage of one year's surplus was an important aspect of subsistence. Utility jars increase in size to allow for the greater quantities of supplies. With such stores of food, the Mimbres could *fig. 29* have withstood a year or two of poor harvests.

29 *Three vessels showing the gradual increase in size and texturing of the Mimbres utility wares.*

There was one important rainfall sequence that did stand out. During the AD 1000s precipitation was above average in many years, and may have allowed the Mimbres to farm in marginal areas. So some dams in the mountains and Classic sites in the desert may have been usable only because of this unusually high rainfall. As the population became excessively large in the early and middle Classic period, the climate was particularly good and allowed for the continued expansion of sites and for movement into marginal areas. The Classic Mimbres population may have been able to expand because of particularly favorable climatic circumstances, even though the rainfall changes were not particularly great.

The tree-ring sequence reveals that during the early AD 1100s the weather pattern was no longer favorable. There were more poor years than before. Under other circumstances this relatively small change in precipitation may not have been disruptive. But the Mimbres population had grown to the point where the resource base was being used to the limit, and the consequences of this drop in rainfall may have been catastrophic. Bad years may have come too close together, causing the exhaustion of stored supplies. This may have led to starvation for a large part of the population, perhaps accompanied by considerable migration out of the Mimbres area in the hope of finding food elsewhere, changes which would have considerably strained the social fabric.

The first few decades of the 1100s may have been traumatic for the Mimbres people. When we remember that their culture disappeared between about AD 1130 and 1150, it is tempting to cite this change in rainfall, coupled with a large population, as the cause of the disappearance. But human cultures are adaptable and resilient, and such a simple explanation should be viewed with caution. The movement of people away from their own lands to live with groups in adjacent regions during particularly bad times would have partly alleviated the problem. But even starvation will not always be accompanied by the collapse of the society. And although the Mimbres clearly had a difficult time in the early AD 1100s, it is far from obvious that this alone destroyed the society.

As we shall see, there are other likely causes for the disappearance of the people. Their difficulty in feeding themselves may have been a severe problem, but it need not have been the sole cause for their society's collapse.

13 The disappearance of the Mimbres

Perhaps our major achievement has been to obtain the first real information on what happened to the Mimbres people. While we are far from fully understanding their disappearance, we are much closer to this than before. It turns out that their demise was probably not solely a product of events in the Mimbres area alone, so it is necessary to consider their relationship to other contemporary peoples of the Southwest in the AD 1000s and 1100s.

Until about AD 1000 the Southwest was occupied by people who lived in relatively small groups of a hundred or less, and whose social organization was not complex. An important break in this pattern of small autonomous villages with simple sociopolitical structures occurred in the center of the Anasazi area in Chaco Canyon. This area, some 225 miles north of the Mimbres heartland, witnessed a flowering of material culture and a sustained and substantial increase in population that resulted in a society unique in the Southwest.

Expansion of the Chaco culture occurred during the AD 1000s and early 1100s. Its center was in Chaco Canyon itself, where over a dozen large towns were constructed, containing many hundreds of rooms each, some blocks standing five stories high. Other buildings dating to the Chaco expansion must have required considerable labor, probably organized by community leaders. Public works included large and elaborate great kivas and other ceremonial structures. A system of dams and canals was constructed to control water for irrigation. Besides the population concentration in the canyon itself, there were over fifty Chacoan communities situated some distance away in all directions. Many of these towns also comprised very large, multistoried pueblos. They extended at least 110 miles from Chaco Canyon itself. Most surprisingly, they were often connected to each other and to the central communities in Chaco Canyon by a system of recently discovered roads. These were sometimes 10 m wide, well constructed and remarkably straight.[37]

The actual nature of Chaco society and political organization and the reasons for its flowering are still the source of considerable debate. Its development in the eleventh and early twelfth centuries may well have been a consequence of its importance in a trading network linking the Anasazi area with Mesoamerica. The presence of large quantities of turquoise and parrots at Chaco Canyon supports this interpretation, as do various architectural traits which have Mesoamerican counterparts. It is not necessary to argue, as some archaeologists have done, that traders from Mexico in residence at Chaco were the cause of the changes. The central Chacoan community's participation in the network may have been sufficient to stimulate the development of regional Chaco society. In fact, many outlying Chacoan communities were perhaps established to facilitate movement along the trade routes, especially the route to the south.[38]

Through this trade network Chacoan society may have established a relationship with the Mimbres. If one wants to carry goods south to Mexico from Chaco Canyon, the most direct route passes through the center of the Mimbres area, where there are no outlying Chacoan communities. It is likely, therefore, that some symbiotic relationship existed between the Chaco and the Mimbres. Most likely, the Mimbres housed and fed the bearers in return for a share in some of the goods being transported. As we have seen, the Mimbres probably received some of the turquoise being carried south to Mexico, and some of the parrots and copper bells coming north. Such a relationship would not imply that the Mimbres were under the domination of the Chacoan culture, but instead were sharing in the fruits of the trade system.

One may ask how was it, if such a trade network did exist, that Mimbres pottery did not also find itself traded along the network? To some extent the Mimbres bowls were indeed widely distributed through trade. However, the finest figurative bowls do not seem to have moved out of the Mimbres area. I suspect that they functioned in Mimbres life in such a way that either the Mimbres would not trade them, or other groups did not want them.

It has long been known that construction and remodeling of the great Chaco towns ended abruptly in about AD 1130. Most of the big towns were almost or completely abandoned and Chaco-style pottery ceased to be produced. While there is no evidence of a major drop in the size of the population, the social organization that was capable of producing these large towns, roads, irrigation works, and so on, seems to have collapsed.[39] Major population relocations did occur throughout the region and the Chacoan society as previously organized no longer existed. Until our work began, it was not realized that the Chaco collapse was concurrent with that of the Mimbres. Most archaeologists have felt that the Mimbres communities survived until much later than is indicated by our tree-ring dates, and that the cultures were not co-terminous. We know now that the Mimbres collapse must have taken place very near AD 1130 as well.[40]

It is extremely unlikely that these major events would have occurred at the same time without being related. This assertion is enhanced by the knowledge that the period between the AD 1130s and 1150s was not generally a time of abandonments or cultural devolution in the Southwest as a whole. Environmental change has frequently been suggested as an explanation for the Chacoan collapse. But it has never been shown that the climate deteriorated significantly at this time in that area. One could claim that the Chaco had been pushing their resource capacity to the limit and even a slight deterioration in the climate would have been enough to cause considerable disruption in the social fabric. This argument is similar to that previously proposed for the Mimbres Valley in the early 1100s, when a small climate shift may have caused considerable resource stress. But except for some pressure on the northern periphery of the Southwest, the rest of the Mogollon and Anasazi areas saw no such sociological declines in this period. There is no tree-ring-derived climatic evidence to suggest that rainfall dropped only in the Chaco and Mimbres areas. Also, why would climate have caused both the Mimbres and Chaco to disappear completely as cultural entities, and not merely to change in less dramatic ways? These possibilities seem only remotely likely, and a sociological explanation appears far more probable.

Recent archaeological work, including some of our own in the Mimbres Valley, has produced evidence for just such a sociological or cultural phenomenon. Immediately to the south of the Mimbres area, and astride the trade route to the south, lies the great prehistoric town of Casas Grandes. This town is larger than any other community in the Southwest. Its massive adobe walls form multistoried rooms numbering into the thousands. Smaller but culturally similar communities surround it. Casas Grandes has long been known to archaeologists, but its role in Southwestern prehistory has remained obscure until recently.

Excavations carried out there by Charles DiPeso in the 1960s have helped to clarify the nature of this community.[41] Two important aspects of the site are now readily apparent. First of all, it was a trading and production center, and quite unlike the prehistoric communities in the rest of the Southwest. Stockpiles of goods, one containing over a million shell beads, were found at Casas Grandes. These goods were procured from a very large area, including shell from both the Pacific and the Caribbean. The craftsmanship in the pottery production and stone work indicates the presence of highly skilled craft specialists. Numerous very well-made copper artifacts occur, and evidence has been found in the form of slag fragments for actual smelting, which would also have required skilled specialists. Production quarters, including an area for raising parrots, perhaps for trade, were also found. There is equally ample evidence that the Casas Grandes community had close ties with Mesoamerican societies to the south. The signs include raised platform mounds, sunken courtyards, and artifacts such as ceramic hand drums, all of which are specifically Mesoamerican and not in the least Southwestern in form.

A major part of the economy of this large community was focused on mercantile activities, to an even greater degree than at Chaco Canyon. Like at Chaco, the society was merely centered at Casas Grandes. A number of settlements, both large and small, were included in a system which extended some 170 miles from the main community. The archaeological evidence indicates that this structure was not the result of gradual evolution, but that it expanded rapidly. Clearly its development must have had considerable consequences over parts of the Southwest, since its economy was in part based on trade with regions to the north.

The question of dating the rise of Casas Grandes is an important one. Opinions vary from the AD 1060s to as late as 1300. Such a wide discrepancy has obviously made it impossible to assess correctly the impact of Casas Grandes.

Today the picture is much clearer. Radiocarbon and tree-ring dates were recovered by DiPeso from Casas Grandes and we obtained supplementary tree-ring and archaeomagnetic dates from sites of the Casas Grandes culture in the Mimbres Valley which contributed to the picture. Contrary to earlier estimates, it now appears that the first major growth of the Casas Grandes system took place in about AD 1130 to 1150.[42] So the demise of the Mimbres and the Chaco cultures coincided with the rise of the Casas Grandes interaction sphere. This information requires a reconsideration of the disappearance of the Mimbres culture. If the previously hypothesized date of AD 1300 for the rise of Casas Grandes is correct, then it would be difficult to argue that there was any connection between that event and the collapse of the Mimbres. If the other hypothesized date of AD 1060 is accepted, then the Casas Grandes culture would be contemporaneous with the Mimbres and Chaco cultures. In neither case would the development of Casas Grandes explain the collapse of the Mimbres and Chaco societies. Now, however, it is clear that the development of the Casas Grandes system was roughly concurrent with the disappearance of the others, strongly suggesting that the events were related.

One model which would account for their contemporaneity is that Chaco and Mimbres societies were symbiotic and non-competitive. The Chacoans traded goods to Mesoamerica, helped by the Mimbreños who acted in some way as middlemen. During this time there was a relatively low density of population in the Casas Grandes region. People lived in small communities and engaged in a little trade. Around AD 1130 these settlements were transformed and expanded rapidly, resulting in the large town of Casas Grandes, which appears to have taken over the role that Chacoans played in the trade to Mesoamerica. Because Casas Grandes is closer to Mesoamerica it was better located to control the trade both to and from Mesoamerica. This led to the quick collapse of the Chaco culture. The total population of the greater Chacoan area, however, did not decrease. The large towns disbanded and the population dispersed. The upper stratum of the social system lost its economic base and the integration of the region broke down.

Under other circumstances, these events would have had minimal impact on the Mimbres who were only involved in this trade to a minor degree. However, the Mimbres lay in the path of the expanding Casas Grandes sphere of influence. By AD 1179, and probably before, villages clearly related to the Casas Grandes culture were built in the Mimbres Valley. This expansion was similar to that seen previously in the Chaco area. A large network of villages was founded in the surrounding regions, probably for the production of food and other commodities needed in the large central communities. In the case of Chacoan expansion these satellite communities seem to have had a minimal impact on the indigenous populations, for they retained their cultural identity. The Casas Grandes expansion differed in this respect, and populations were incorporated into the Casas Grandes system. Besides the Mimbres area, peoples in southeast Arizona and much of north Chihuahua were also drawn into the dominant society. The archaeological remains found in these areas at this time are similar in many ways to the material culture of Casas Grandes.

How the Mimbres culture was made to disappear we do not know. Were all of the Mimbres people incorporated into the Casas Grandes cultural system, or did some move into other parts of the Southwest beyond the Casas Grandes region? Was this assimilation by choice or by force? And what happened to the people?

These questions are not easy to answer using current archaeological information, but we do have some partial answers. First of all, we need to consider the state of Mimbres culture at about AD 1130. We have seen that population increases within the area, coupled with a less favorable rainfall regime, placed the subsistence economy in a precarious position. A series of crop failures may have resulted in famine and population decline, maybe accompanied by migration out of the area. This would have left the valley ripe for colonization by the Casas Grandes people.

Such a scenario is quite plausible given what we know about the Mimbres in the AD 1100s, and what we know of the effects of famine from elsewhere in the world. But it is difficult to demonstrate that famine was indeed involved, or that the Mimbres were incapable of sustaining themselves. An alternative view would be that they had some difficult years toward the end of the eleventh century and the beginning of the twelfth century, but that their society was still viable in AD 1130. If this was the case, the Mimbres population may perhaps have been displaced, or at least the valley incorporated into the Casas Grandes sphere, for other reasons and by other methods.

Perhaps the Mimbres population was induced to become part of the Casas Grandes interaction sphere because of apparent advantages in belonging to such an elaborate and complex organization. Similar processes are occurring around the world today; peasant populations are migrating to large cities because of real or perceived advantages of living in these centers. Nevertheless, we must remember that traditional tribal societies like the Mimbres are inherently conservative and are not likely to change their way of life willingly.

It may be that the Mimbres were neither decimated by famine nor that they voluntarily joined the Casas Grandes system. The outsiders may instead have moved into the area by threatened or actual force, and the population forcibly required to participate in the new system, possibly through resettlement in the central Casas Grandes area.

With these possibilities in mind, we conducted limited excavations on sites related to the Casas Grandes cultural system found in the Mimbres Valley. We were particularly interested in how such sites differed from Classic Mimbres ones, and in the dates of the Casas Grandes-related sites. The period of domination extended from *c.* 1150 to 1300, and has been called the Black Mountain phase, after a concentration of sites of this period along the lower Mimbres River in the desert area not far from a small volcanic remnant of that name. Even though people who occupied these sites now seem to us to have had a close cultural and economic relationship with the population at and around Casas Grandes, we felt this new name was useful to distinguish the inhabitants of the Mimbres area from those of Casas Grandes itself.

Our most important excavations for this period were undertaken on the Walsh site.[43] This village is located at the lower (southern) end of the Mimbres Valley, in an area heavily used by Black Mountain phase people. This area is more than 300 m lower than the Galaz and Mattocks sites, so is much hotter in the summertime. Excavating there was such hot work that heat exhaustion might have been a problem. But the rooms were not too deep and the soil was soft.

Unfortunately, the Walsh site had been severely damaged by looters, even though it did not contain Mimbres pottery. By the time we began excavations there during the third field season, our skill in salvaging information from vandalized sites had greatly improved, and we quickly found undamaged portions of the village. Unlike the Mimbres sites, the Black Mountain pueblos were built of adobe. The walls were constructed not of bricks, but by puddling wet adobe into courses about 30 cm high. Each course was allowed to dry before another was added.

The Walsh site was a U-shaped pueblo. Each side of the U consisted of several rows of rooms, and the U opened toward the Mimbres River. The village contained about sixty rooms. We could find no evidence of either kivas or ramadas, in contrast to Mimbres villages of this size. After the site was abandoned, the roofs collapsed and the walls began to be eroded by rain and snow. The rooms soon became filled with melted adobe, the same material as the remaining portions of the standing walls. This makes adobe walls hard to find and to excavate; differences in hardness and slight color changes are used to locate the standing walls, which otherwise tend to look just like the surrounding soil.

We located and excavated four rooms at the Walsh site, as well as areas within the plaza and outside the pueblo. Room 10 was particularly significant. This was a living room with a hearth and a central roof-support post. After it had been in use for some time it was burned. The room was later rebuilt; a new floor was laid above the original floor, and a new hearth was built. For a second time the room burned, and a third floor and hearth were constructed. We used the new archaeomagnetic technique to date these three hearths. The original hearth, which we knew must have been the earliest, was dated to AD 1250, the middle hearth to 1255, and the uppermost and latest one to 1270. Dating hearths with such accuracy is a remarkable achievement for so new a technique.[44] The dates were very helpful in establishing the time range of the Black Mountain phase. We conducted more limited excavations on two other Black Mountain phase sites. Burned rooms at the Montoya site produced tree-ring dates of AD 1179.

As we began to understand the nature of these sites, we realized that there had been occupations of this time range at several of the Classic Mimbres villages. For example, at the Galaz site a block of rooms had been built on top of collapsed Mimbres structures. Pottery and architectural details suggest that this room block was constructed during the Black Mountain phase. At other Mimbres sites, evidence of use during the Black Mountain phase is usually more limited; their post-Mimbres occupations were apparently brief and small. On the basis of all this information we were able to reconstruct several pieces of community life at this period.

The post-Mimbres occupation of the valley took two forms. There was some reuse of the old village locations of the Classic period. We currently believe this took place at the beginning of the Black Mountain phase of occupation in the valley. Deposits are mixed with those of the Classic Mimbres period, and we do not know much about them. Apparently somewhat later, new villages began to be built elsewhere. Almost all were in the lower end of the valley, and the upper end was almost completely abandoned. These villages were constructed of adobe and range from about a dozen up to several hundred rooms. The total population of the valley was less than half of what it had been during the Classic Mimbres period.

The settlements were strikingly different from their Classic Mimbres predecessors. Rooms were considerably larger, and incorporated a new design of roof-support. Even the hearths were different from the Mimbres stone-lined rectangular ones; those of Black Mountain houses were adobe bowls of such small proportions that it is hard to see how they could have used firewood in them. The artifacts are also different, and few pottery types of the Classic plate 38 Mimbres period are found; only some utility wares show some similarities. plate 36 The painted wares found at Black Mountain sites are generally inferior in craftsmanship to Mimbres pottery, and although some of the geometric designs are similar, the figurative renditions that are the glory of Mimbres work are completely absent.

The burial customs present an even more enigmatic picture. Unlike in the Mimbres sites, both burials and cremations occurred in almost equal numbers. The burials were strikingly similar to the previous Mimbres ones, with bodies interred beneath the floors of rooms in a flexed position, and a 'killed' bowl was inverted over the head. The only difference is that various pottery types were used instead of Mimbres bowls. Cremations were also interred beneath room floors; burned and calcinated bones were placed in a jar which was then covered with an inverted bowl. A few burials have been found without grave goods and with the skulls missing, suggesting that the bodies were decapitated before being interred, something unknown in Mimbres villages.

Overall, these sites bear no close resemblance to Mimbres sites, with substantial changes in architecture, burial customs, artifacts, and site locations. Yet beneath the surface one sees many small things, like some of the burial customs, that are very recognizably Mimbres. From this wealth of rather disparate information we can draw several conclusions.

We have seen that the Classic Mimbres disappeared around AD 1130, and that Black Mountain people were constructing new villages no later than 1179. These sites continued to be occupied at least up to 1270, but we find no evidence that they existed after 1300. Since our excavations in Black Mountain phase deposits were very limited, it is extremely unlikely that the earliest tree-ring dates we obtained were from the first Black Mountain village in the valley. So we can assume that this new occupation quickly followed the demise of the Mimbres, and probably began around 1150.

From archaeological research in other areas we know that the Mimbres did not move as a group to other regions to continue their traditions there. It is possible and even likely, however, that several small groups of Mimbres people did join some of the groups to the north and east of the Mimbres. But they must have assimilated quickly, because there is no archaeological evidence of their Mimbres heritage. As it seems unlikely that all the Mimbres died out at this time, we must conclude that at least some were incorporated by some means into the Casas Grandes culture.

We now suspect that soon after the founding of Casas Grandes, satellite communities were established over a wide area. These villages probably provided labor, food, and other commodities for the large towns of the central area. The Mimbres region was selected as one of those to be exploited, and the Black Mountain population was settled in the southern end of the valley, living in large adobe pueblos. This area is even today favorable for growing cotton, so the settlements may have been founded in order to supply this commodity to the central community.

The Casas Grandes people probably used several methods to integrate the Mimbres into their culture. The cremations found in these sites may represent the presence of a non-Mimbres population in the valley. The reshuffling of communities may have served to break down old cultural traditions. The same motive may also have led to the disappearance of the Mimbres art tradition. If the bowls were significant in a religion which was not like that practiced at Casas Grandes, then the ceramic tradition may have been eliminated precisely in order to integrate the Mimbres into the new culture. Thus the majority of the Mimbres may have survived the Casas Grandes expansion, but without their culture.

Once the Mimbres became absorbed by the Casas Grandes, or joined with other groups to the north and east, they cannot be traced archaeologically. The Casas Grandes system lasted only about 150 years and then collapsed. Many of the participants subsequently moved north into the Mogollon area. These groups probably included descendants of the Classic Mimbres people.

During the 1300s and 1400s there was considerable population decline and movement out of the Mogollon region.[45] When the first Spanish Conquistadores reached the area, most of it had been abandoned.

It is possible that some of the descendants of the Mimbres eventually joined the Zuni, the Acoma, or other historic Pueblo communities, but we cannot establish any direct line of descent. Many Mimbres motifs are used even today by Puebloan potters, but this is purely a result of copying the Mimbres painted bowls which have been recovered by archaeologists.

14 Reflections

The five years of fieldwork by the Mimbres Foundation have drawn to a close, and we are now in the process of producing detailed technical reports on our work. Although we know a great deal more about the Mimbres than we used to, there is certainly much that remains to be discovered. In the case of the pottery, our chances of making new breakthroughs are quite good. The Mimbres Archive is still in its infancy, and its photos of 6500 bowls are surely capable of yielding fresh data on the Mimbres way of life.

One cannot be quite so optimistic about our learning more about other aspects of Mimbres prehistory. Some sites still have undisturbed deposits, but the majority are completely destroyed or very badly damaged. There may have been only one settlement like the Galaz site. And now even that is gone, together with the information that was unique to it.

The Mimbres Foundation, however, turned out to have far wider-reaching effects than were ever intended on the preservation of prehistoric cultures all over the United States. Any sites on government land were always protected by law, but the vast majority are on private land and receive no legal protection whatsoever from destruction. The Mimbres Foundation initially dealt with this problem in a traditional way. We tried to excavate threatened sites before they were destroyed. Such complete excavation is not a very desirable way of recovering information, since archaeologists are constantly improving their methods and hence their ability to learn from sites. Many of our techniques were not available even ten years before. Thus, the goal usually is to ensure that some sites are left intact for future archaeologists.

The total excavation of threatened Mimbres sites was thus not the best long-term solution. Nor was it practical. The bulldozers that uncovered Mimbres burials and their bowls moved quickly, and it was impossible to keep ahead of them. We finally had to change our approach. We found that sites in the Mimbres area could be purchased for a fraction of the cost of excavating them. Thus, with the same resources we could acquire and preserve many more sites than we could excavate. The only way to ensure that Classic Mimbres pueblos are preserved for future generations is to have them permanently held and protected by public institutions for that specific purpose. It is difficult for a private individual who owns property on which an archaeological site is located to ensure its protection for posterity, no matter how good his intentions.

The foundation's strategy copes with this reality. We have successfully acquired a number of sites; for the first time prehistoric villages in the Mimbres Valley are permanently safeguarded. Although the Galaz site is gone completely, the Mattocks site is now guarded and will be studied and enjoyed by many generations in the future.

It was apparent that this problem was not restricted to the Mimbres Valley. Many important sites elsewhere in the United States were lost each year to vandalism, land development, and other forces. Board members of the Mimbres Foundation, other archaeologists, and conservationists, formed the Archaeological Conservancy to deal with this problem on a national scale.[46] This is a non-profit-making foundation which actively preserves important prehistoric and historic ruins throughout the United States. Projects recently completed by the Conservancy include an early-man site over 10,000 years old and an historic site of the last century. Sites have been protected from the Ohio Valley to the Pacific coast. So research by the Mimbres Foundation in southwestern New Mexico has resulted not only in further understanding of the Mimbres, but in the preservation of sites across the country.

Our research has also provided insights into the behavior of prehistoric societies in general. When we look at the Mimbres relationship with their natural environment, we see on the one hand that it was very close and interrelated. On the other hand, however, we have seen that this was not always in balance. The prehistoric Mimbres, like man today, overexploited their environment, causing changes in the plant and animal communities.

Archaeologists working nearby and in other regions of the world are finding that the behavior of prehistoric populations was not always optimal for the environment. These early peoples were fully capable of causing deleterious effects, and some did.

If we look at the Mimbres case, we see that the Mimbres population grew until it was overexploiting certain limited resources and becoming increasingly at risk. The growth was apparently not substantially controlled even though these resources were being overused. Cultural mechanisms to limit growth may have been instituted by the Mimbres, but they seem not to have been effective. This shows that knowledge of the environment and a close relationship with it do not guarantee that man can live in long-term equilibrium with nature. There are no inherent built-in mechanisms that keep human population in balance with nature.

The difference between the effects of prehistoric peoples on the environment and those of modern populations is really one of degree. The Mimbres, like many other prehistoric peoples, did not have a complex technology or large population densities. So their ability to damage the environment was limited. They stripped the river floodplain of trees for firewood and overexploited the deer population. Other examples of their modification of the natural environment, however, show the limitations of their impact. The technology available to them to control water and erosion, by constructing check dams in

the upper sections of semi-permanent tributaries of the Mimbres River, had no appreciable effects. After the population declined, the environment returned to the natural condition in which it had been prior to the arrival of the Classic Mimbres. The plant and animal communities had not been so damaged that regeneration was impossible.

Today in the Mimbres Valley man is again modifying the landscape to suit his immediate needs. This time, however, the effects are much greater and not so easily reversed. Because of the overgrazing of pasturage, the hillslopes on either side of the valley are less able to retain rainfall. With this decrease in moisture retention, the river is more prone to flood, and when it overflows its banks causes erosion of fields and the washing out of bridges. Most people now believe this to be a natural condition of the river, and that it always flooded this way. We know from the archaeology that this is not true. One reaction to the current problem of frequent severe flooding has been to straighten the channel with bulldozers. This has caused the water to flow faster and deeper than ever before. Already, three plant species and two animal species are no longer to be found in the drainage. We have firm archaeological evidence that these plants and animals were present during the Classic Mimbres period. They needed slow-running or ponded water; their disappearance can be attributed to the effects of modern population on the riverine habitat.

Modern man, then, is not inherently more or less destructive than prehistoric peoples. Today, as prehistorically, the natural environment is modified without considering the long-term consequences. Today, however, we are much more liable to cause irreversible damage because of our greater numbers and more powerful technology. Archaeology has an important role to play in helping man to understand and use the natural environment properly. Information on earlier populations and environments can help us understand what changes have taken place in the past. Archaeology can provide knowledge of the past which is not only interesting in its own right, but which can also help us understand what is happening to us today. It is easy to enjoy knowing about the history of the Mimbres people and to appreciate their art. We can learn from them as well.

Chronological table

AD	
	Post-Mimbres (Casas Grandes related)
1130	
	The Classic Mimbres period
1000	
	Three Circle phase
	The Late Pithouse period
	San Francisco phase
	Georgetown phase
550	
	The Early Pithouse period
200	
	Archaic hunters and gatherers

Chronology for the Mimbres area. A major transformation in life-style occurred at AD 200, when permanent structures and pottery became common during the Early Pithouse period. The Late Pithouse period (traditionally divided into three phases) saw the beginning of painted ceramics. The Classic Mimbres period witnessed the shift to surface pueblos, the elaboration of ceramic art and the peak of population. The post-Mimbres period showed radical changes in architecture and pottery as well as a drop in population. These new characteristics were related to the growing influence of the large town of Casas Grandes in northern Mexico.

Notes

Chapter 2

1 Edward H. Spicer, *Cycles of Conquest*, University of Arizona Press, Tucson, 1962.
2 Edward P. Dozier, *The Pueblo Indians of North America*, Holt, Rinehart and Winston, New York, 1970.
3 Translated by George P. Hammond and Agapito Rey, *The Rediscovery of New Mexico 1580–1594*, University of New Mexico Press, Albuquerque, 1966.
4 Richard I. Ford, *An Ecological Analysis Involving the Population of San Juan Pueblo, New Mexico*, PhD Dissertation, University of Michigan, 1968.
5 John C. McGregor, *Southwestern Archaeology*, University of Illinois Press, Urbana, 2nd edn, 1965. H. Marie Wormington, *Prehistoric Indians of the Southwest*, Denver Museum of Natural History Popular Series 7, 5th edn, 1961.
6 Paul E. Minnis, *Economic and Organizational Responses to Food Stress by Nonstratified Societies: An Example from Prehistoric New Mexico*, PhD Dissertation, University of Michigan, 1981.

Chapter 3

7 Steven A. LeBlanc and Michael E. Whalen, *An Archaeological Synthesis of South-Central and Southwestern New Mexico*, Office of Contract Archeology, University of New Mexico, 1980.
8 Jesse W. Fewkes, 'Animal Figures in Prehistoric Pottery from the Mimbres Valley, New Mexico', *American Anthropologist* 18 (4), 1916, pp. 535–45. Jesse W. Fewkes, 'Designs on Prehistoric Pottery from the Mimbres Valley, New Mexico', *Smithsonian Miscellaneous Collections* 74 (6), Washington DC, 1923. Jesse W. Fewkes, 'Additional Designs on Prehistoric Mimbres Pottery', *Smithsonian Miscellaneous Collections* 76 (8), Washington DC, 1924.

9 Wesley Bradfield, *Cameron Creek Village, A Site in the Mimbres Area in Grant County, New Mexico*, The School of American Research, Santa Fe, 1929.
10 H.S. and C.B. Cosgrove, 'The Swarts Ruin, a Typical Mimbres Site in Southwestern New Mexico', *Papers of the Peabody Museum of American Archaeology and Ethnology, Harvard University* 15 (1), 1932.
11 Bruce Bryan, 'Excavations of the Galaz Ruin', *The Masterkey* 4 (6), 1931, pp. 179–89. Bruce Bryan, 'Excavations of the Galaz Ruin', *The Masterkey* 4 (7), 1931, pp. 221–26.
12 Paul H. Nesbitt, 'The Ancient Mimbreños, Based on Investigations at the Mattocks Ruin, Mimbres Valley, New Mexico', *Logan Museum Bulletin* 4, 1931.
13 Emil W. Haury, 'The Mogollon Culture of Southwestern New Mexico', *Medallion Papers* 20, Globe, Arizona, 1936.

Chapter 4

14 Roger Anyon, Patricia A. Gilman, and Steven A. LeBlanc, 'A Re-evaluation of the Mimbres-Mogollon Sequence', *The Kiva* 46 (4), 1981, pp. 209–25.
15 Steven A. LeBlanc, *Mimbres Archaeological Center: Preliminary Report of the First Season of Excavation, 1974*, The Institute of Archaeology, University of California, Los Angeles, 1975. Steven A. LeBlanc, 'The 1976 Field Season of the Mimbres Foundation in Southwestern New Mexico', *Journal of New World Archaeology* 2 (2), 1977, pp. 1–24.

Chapter 5

16 Robert W. Keyser, 'The Architecture of the Galaz Site', MA Dissertation, University of Minnesota, 1965. James Provinzano, 'The Osteological Remains of the Galaz Mimbres Amerinds', MA Disser-

tation, University of Minnesota, 1968.

17 Our population estimates are derived by using Casselberry's floor area to population ratio. Samuel E. Casselberry, 'Further Refinement of Formulas for Determining Population from Floor Area', *World Archaeology* 6 (1), 1974, pp. 117–22.

Chapter 6

18 Roger Anyon and Steven A. LeBlanc, 'The Architectural Evolution of Mogollon-Mimbres Communal Structures', *The Kiva* 45, 1980, pp. 253–77.

Chapter 7

19 Emil W. Haury, 'Some Southwestern Pottery Types Series IV', *Medallion Papers* 19, Globe, Arizona, 1936.

20 Emil W. Haury, *The Hohokam: Desert Farmers and Craftsmen, Excavations at Snaketown, 1964–1965*, University of Arizona Press, 1976. H.S. Gladwin, Emil W. Haury, Edwin B. Sayles, and Nora Gladwin, 'Excavations at Snaketown, Material Culture', *Medallion Papers* 25, Globe, Arizona, 1937.

21 See Brody for a discussion of influences on Mimbres pottery. J.J. Brody, *Mimbres Painted Pottery*, University of New Mexico Press, 1977.

Chapter 8

22 Anyon, Gilman, and LeBlanc 1980, *op. cit.* n. 13.

23 Steven A. LeBlanc, 'Mimbres Archaeological Center, Preliminary Report of the Second Season of Excavations, 1975', *Journal of New World Archaeology* 1 (6), 1976, pp. 1–23. LeBlanc 1975 and 1977, *op. cit.* n. 14. LeBlanc and Whalen 1980, *op. cit.* n. 6.

Chapter 9

25 Ben A. Nelson, Margaret C. Rugge, and Steven A. LeBlanc, 'A Small Classic Mimbres Ruin in the Mimbres Valley', in, A.E. Ward (ed.), *Limited Activity and Occupational Sites: A Collection of Conference Papers*, Centre for Anthropological Studies, Albuquerque, New Mexico, 1978.

26 C.B. Cosgrove, 'Two Kivas at Treasure Hill', *El Palacio* 15 (2), 1923, pp. 19–21.

27 Anyon and LeBlanc 1980, *op. cit.* n. 17.

28 Fred Eggan, *The Social Organization of the Western Pueblos*, University of Chicago Press, Chicago, 1950.

Chapter 10

29 See Brody 1977, *op. cit.* n. 20, for a detailed discussion of Mimbres pottery.

30 For an earlier Hopi interpretation of Mimbres bowls see Fred Kabotie, *Designs from the Ancient Mimbreños with a Hopi Interpretation*, Graborn Press, San Francisco, 1949.

31 C.B. Cosgrove, 'Caves of the Upper Gila and Hueco Area in New Mexico and Texas', *Papers of the Peabody Museum of American Archaeology and Ethnology, Harvard University* 24 (2), 1947. George H. Pepper, 'Pueblo Bonito', *American Museum of Natural History, Anthropological Papers* 27, 1920.

Chapter 11

32 Such a sash is on display at the museum at Mesa Verde National Park, Colorado.

33 Harry J. Shafer, A.J. Taylor, and Steve J. Usrey, 'Archaeological Investigation at the NAN (Hinton) Ranch Ruin, Grant County, New Mexico', *Anthropology Laboratory Special Series* 3, Texas A and M University, College Station, Texas, 1979.

34 See Elman R. Service, *Primitive Social Organization*, Random House, NY, 1962, for a discussion of the concepts employed here.

Chapter 12

35 Details of the information used in this chapter are given in Minnis 1981, *op. cit.* n. 5 and Paul E. Minnis, 'Paleoethnobotanical Indicators of Prehistoric Environmental Disturbance; A Case Study', in, R. Ford (ed.), *The Nature and Status of Ethnobotany*, University of Michigan Museum of Anthropology, Anthropological Papers 67, Ann Arbor, 1978, pp. 347–66.

36 Jeffry S. Dean and William J. Robinson, *Expanded Tree-Ring Chronology for the*

Southwestern United States, University of Arizona Laboratory of Tree-Ring Research Chronology Series 3, Tuscon, 1978.

Chapter 13

37 A large number of unpublished manuscripts on Chaco Canyon are on file at the Chaco Center, National Park Service, University of New Mexico. The most readily available works include: Paul Grebinger, 'Prehistoric social organization in Chaco Canyon, New Mexico: An Alternative Reconstruction', *The Kiva* 39 (1): 3–23. Michael P. Marshall, John R. Stein, Richard W. Loose, and Judith E. Novotny, *Anasazi Communities of the San Juan Basin*, Public Service Company of New Mexico and The Historic Preservation Bureau, State of New Mexico, Santa Fe, 1979. Neil M. Judd, 'Material Culture of Pueblo Bonito', *Smithsonian Miscellaneous Collections* 124, Washington DC, 1954. Neil M. Judd, 'The Architecture of Pueblo Bonito', *Smithsonian Miscellaneous Collections* 147 (1), Washington DC, 1964.

38 See various papers in Riley, Carroll, and Basil Hedricks, *Across the Chichimec Sea*, Southern Illinois Press, Carbondale, 1978. Edwin N. Ferdon Jr, *A Trial Survey of Mexican-Southwestern Architectural Parallels*, School of American Research Monographs 21, 1955. But see an alternative viewpoint in Randall H. McGuire, 'The Mesoamerican Connection in the South-west', *The Kiva* 46 (1 and 2), 1980, pp. 3–38.

39 Tree-ring dates can be found for Chaco sites in: Bryan Bannister, William J. Robinson, and Richard L. Warren, *Tree-ring dates from New Mexico A, G–H: Shiprock-Zuni-Mt. Taylor*, University of Arizona Laboratory of Tree-ring Research, Tucson, 1970. William J. Robinson, Bruce J. Harrell, and Richard L. Warren, *Tree-ring Dates from New Mexico B: Chaco-Gobernador area*, University of Arizona Laboratory of Tree-ring Research, Tucson, 1974.

40 Steven A. LeBlanc, 'The Dating of Casas Grandes', *American Antiquity* 45 (4), 1980, pp. 779–805.

41 Charles DiPeso, John B. Rinaldo, and Gloria J. Fenner, 'Casas Grandes: A Fallen Trading Center of the Gran Chichimeca', *Amerind Foundation Publication* 9 (1–8), Northland Press, Flagstaff, Arizona, 1974.

42 Steven A. LeBlanc 1980, *op. cit.* n. 38.

43 Steven A. LeBlanc 1977, *op. cit.* n. 14.

44 The samples were taken by Dr David Doyel and analyzed by Dr Jeffrey Eighmy.

45 David E. Doyel, and Emil W. Haury, 'The 1976 Salado Conference', *The Kiva* 42 (1), 1976.

Chapter 14

46 Mark P. Michel, 'Preserving America's Prehistoric Heritage'. *Archaeology* 34 (2), 1981, pp. 61–63.

Bibliography

BRADFIELD, Wesley, *Cameron Creek Village, A site in the Mimbres Area in Grant County, New Mexico*, The School of American Research, Santa Fe, 1929.

BRODY, J.J. *Mimbres Painted Pottery*, University of New Mexico Press, Albuquerque, 1977.

COSGROVE, H.S. and C.B. *The Swarts Ruin, A Typical Mimbres Site in Southwestern New Mexico*, Papers of the Peabody Museum of American Archaeology and Ethnology, Harvard University 15(1), 1932.

LeBLANC, Steven A. 'Mimbres Pottery', Archaeology Magazine, Vol. 31, no. 3, pp. 7–13, 1978.

NESBITT, Paul H. *The Ancient Mimbrenos, Based on Investigations at the Mattocks Ruin, Mimbres Valley, New Mexico*, Logan Museum Bulletin Number 4, 1931.

Acknowledgments

The work of the Mimbres Foundation has been assisted by so many people that it is impossible to thank them all. We would like to thank Ed Janss, Jay Last, Laura Lee Sterns, Christophe DeMenil and John Elliot for their support. The National Science Foundation, the National Endowment for the Humanities, the National Endowment for the Arts, the Janss Foundation and the Rockefeller Brothers Fund gave grants for various aspects of the research described here. The association of the Foundation with the Maxwell Museum, University of New Mexico, has been invaluable. This work would not have been possible without the cooperation and the interest of residents of the Mimbres Valley who assisted us in a variety of ways, but who are too numerous to mention individually. Finally I would like to thank Catherine LeBlanc and J. J. Brody for their reading and comments on the manuscript.

List of illustrations

I would like to thank the following institutions for permission to reproduce photographs and artifacts: Department of Anthropology, University of Minnesota, Minneapolis, Minnesota (UM); Heard Museum, Phoenix, Arizona (HM); Janss Foundation, Thousand Oaks, California (JF); Logan Museum, Beloit College, Beloit, Wisconsin (LM); Maxwell Museum, University of New Mexico, Albuquerque, New Mexico (MM); Mesa Verde National Park, Colorado (MV); Museum of New Mexico, Santa Fe, New Mexico (MNM); National Anthropological Archive, National Museum of Natural History, Smithsonian Institution, Washington DC (SI); Peabody Museum, Harvard University, Cambridge, Massachusetts (PM); School of American Research collection in the Museum of New Mexico, Santa Fe, New Mexico (SAR/MNM); and University Museum, University of Colorado, Boulder, Colorado (UC).

Photographs of bowls are mostly from the Mimbres Archive (MA), for which registration numbers are given here. The majority were taken by Katherine White and Maria Bauer. Other photographs were taken either by the staff of the Mimbres Foundation (MF), or as noted.

Figures

Drawn by Gigi Bayless, except for 6 and 8 which are by Lou Ann Jordan.

Index

Figure numbers appear in **bold** and plates in *italic*.

pottery (*see also* Mimbres bowls)
  corrugated 74, 144, **16**, **26**, *19, 34, 37*
  Early Pithouse period 40, 42–43, *7*
  Late Pithouse period **16**, *34–35, 37*
  Mimbres 116–19, **26**
  post-Mimbres 164, *36, 38*
  utility **29**, *see also* corrugated

rabbits 155
radiocarbon dates 39–40, 67
ramada 82, 85
Rio Mimbres, *see* Mimbres River

San Francisco
  phase 59
  Red pottery 72
San Lorenzo 47
sash 141, *VI, 84*
settlement patterns 150–51, 153
shell 29
site destruction 11–12, 14, 163, *7*
social organization 110, 147
Southwest Museum 30, 47
storage rooms 85, *22*
subsistence 24, 42, 106, 140, 149–57
Swarts site 29–31, 108, 111, **2**, *22–24*

sword, *see* wand

terraces, *see* dams
Thompson site 40–41, 45
Three Circle
  phase 59
  Red on White 73, 116, *VIII, XII*
  site 30
trade 142–43, 159
Treasure Hill **2**
tree-ring dating 15, 25–27, 62, 156, 159, 161, **4**
turquoise 141, 143, 147, 158, *III*

University of Minnesota 30, 47, 58–59, **25**, *9–11*

Walsh site 163–64
wand 120, 139, *XIII, 32, 71, 76*
warfare 45, 76
Webster, Clement 29
Weslowski, Lois 119
Wheaton-Smith site 47, 114, *23*
White, Katherine 57

Zuni 166, *2–4*